S0-EHX-487

Big Wallet, No Pants!

What every young person should know, and most adults have forgotten, about their minds, their money and driving bright red Ferraris.

By

Robert Bakke

Much of this book is a work of fiction. Many places, events, and situations in this story are purely fictional. Any resemblance to actual persons, living or dead, may be coincidental.

© 2003 by Robert Bakke. All rights reserved.

No part of this book may be reproduced, stored in a retrieval system, or transmitted by any means, electronic, mechanical, photocopying, recording, or otherwise, without written permission from the author.

ISBN: 1-4107-2420-4 (e-book)
ISBN: 1-4107-2421-2 (Paperback)

This book is printed on acid free paper.

WITHDRAWN

1stBooks - rev. 10/10/03

Table of Contents

To Meghan and Robbie. You opened my eyes and my heart, and touched my life in ways I could not have imagined. My love for you is unconditional, unlimited, and forever.

Ghost-Phobia

An introduction

So I'm a spirit. Get over it. After all, what do you think that deep down, *you* are? The reality of it is, that the only difference between you and me is the fact that I can *see you*, but you can't see…

Listen, when I lived on earth I was just like you. I even had a name, "Dave Thomas." (No relation to that Wendy's Hamburger guy.) But that was then, and to be honest with you I never really liked being called "Dave" to begin with. However, since you'll have to call me *something* and since humans can't pronounce the name I have now, hummm.

This could present a problem.

Well, no it won't. Just refer to me as "Uncle Bob." Yea, that will work. It's simple, and offers a certain *avuncular* quality that little humans should enjoy. It's perfect. From now on you can refer to me as the spirit of "Uncle Bob." Unless of course you happen to be someone who doesn't believe in spirits. In that case, let me say it like this, *"BOO!"*

Maybe now you'll believe me.

Can't Find Your First Million?

(You were just sitting on it a moment ago.)

Perhaps you should take a few minutes and go through your wallet. After all, a lot of people go through their wallets, and do you know what they find? They find cash, credit cards, a driver's license, old receipts, deposit slips from six months ago, and for a lucky few, an extra ten-dollar bill! "TEN BUCKS!" they yell as though the money had somehow, perhaps magically, been placed there for them to find. But do you know what? They haven't "found" a ten-dollar bill. Finding it implies it had been "lost." But it hadn't been lost. It is a ten-dollar bill, an *asset* that I made them *forget they had*. I've probably made you forget a lot of your assets, also.

For instance, what about all of those creative ideas you used to have? Wouldn't you consider a great idea an asset?

What about your enthusiasm? Enthusiasm is one of your most *powerful* sources of energy and motivation, so wouldn't that qualify as an asset?

What about your dreams, and the *thrill* you feel when you imagine yourself achieving them? Are they assets? Of course they are.

When you take time to consider the things that are most important, you discover that your most valuable assets are the assets that you carry around in your *minds*, as opposed to your wallets. Fortunately for me, when I stop you from putting your assets to use, just like that ten-dollar bill, you tend to forget they are there, and that makes them easy to take away from you.

Don't you ever wonder what happened to all those childhood dreams you used to have? You know the ones. The dreams that people referred to as "just another phase" you were going through?

What about those great new inventions and creative ideas that other people said were *impossible*? The ideas that they called, "crazy."

Remember now? Do you really believe that *friends* just naturally say such discouraging things to each other?

Consider this. Suppose you weren't going through a phase. Suppose your ideas were not all that crazy? Suppose those people who called your ideas *crazy*, or *impossible*, never really intended to say such things.

I would be willing to bet that at least one time in your life you have reached into the pocket of an old pair of jeans and found a couple old dollars that you had forgotten about.

Doesn't it make you wonder what else you have forgotten?

Doesn't it make you wonder, why?

Perhaps you should look up the definition of, *avuncular*.

An Idea In Your Mind is like a Ferrari In The Garage

(But will you get the chance to drive it?)

If I win, Poof! They will be gone. Wasted. Like a Ferrari in the garage that never curved its way down a winding country road, so it will be with your intellectual assets. The thoughts, ideas and ambitions that had put the *thrill* into your eyes will have moved from *your* mind, into *my* bank account, because that's what I do. I find creative ways of stopping you from using your most valuable assets, and then I sneak them away from you.

Sneaking away and bankrolling assets has given me the biggest wallet in the universe. But let's be clear about something. Just because I am a wealthy spirit doesn't make me a mean or destructive one. For example, I have never *once* hidden under a bed hoping to scare a little human! And you won't catch me wearing any of those masks like the ones you see in B-rate scary movies. Would *you* wear one of those things? Finally, you should know that I don't cause p*hysical* harm to anyone. I don't deal in drugs, alcohol, violence or any other form of physical control like some of the other spirits do. I may be a little greedy and a bit of a prankster, but I have never been mean or evil.

The long and the short of it, is that my mission is to make you waste as much of your inherent potential as possible, ultimately preventing you from achieving the things in your life that, deep down, *you know you are supposed to.* Basically, I control your mind *today,* costing you your *fortune* tomorrow. And as you'll learn, I control the minds of the people around you, also.

In the interest of being fair and giving credit, yes, some of you occasionally manage to defeat my efforts. When that happens I pay out accordingly. But hey, it's like being the owner of a Las Vegas casino. I take in millions, and pay out an occasional ten or twenty. Big deal.

Today I have traveled the universe, acquired wealth beyond the kings and possess intellect and athletic ability that exceeds your wildest imagination. Perhaps that is why I've decided to come out into the open. Like a magician who decides to tell the world how he does his tricks and then moves on to something new. Well, I guess I have decided to tell a few secrets of my own. The best part for you is, my doing this will inadvertently be showing you ways to build the fortune that you should have been building all along. But why should I care if you become more successful? I've already made, very quietly, more than I need.

It's time for me to tell a few secrets, sell a few books and then it's off to the links! That's right, we play golf here. And where *we* play, 400-yard tee shots are not out of the question. But then again, Tiger Woods is almost doing that on earth right now.

That guy never listens to a word I say.

The Shoelace of a Rich Man

One of the games I like to play is to make *bright, ambitious* people spend their time doing *silly* and *unproductive* things. Then I have you do them over and over, again and again. This allows me to keep taking and taking, and taking again. It's a process of wealth building and *duplication* very similar to the one Ray Kroc used when he built his McDonald's Hamburger fortune. He found something that worked, and then he did it over and over, again and again. The only difference between Ray's duplication process and the one I use is that his was on a "bright and ambitious" agenda, as opposed to the "silly and unproductive" agenda that I put people on.

For instance, consider the simple snapping of your shoelace. This may not seem like much, but take a look at the big picture.

While tying your shoelace you notice it is beginning to *fray*. What would you think is going to happen very soon? The shoelace is going to *snap*, correct? But what do you do? You tie the lace and forget all about it. Later, you tie the shoelace again, and again notice the fraying. So what do you do? You forget about it, *again*. Later, you tie the shoelace and notice it is fraying worse! But what do you do? You tie it *again* and forget all about it! Like I said earlier, "duplication."

Here are a few questions for you.

Question #1. After noticing that your last broken shoelace was fraying, how many times were you *in* or *near* a store that sells shoelaces but *failed* to purchase new ones?

Question #2. Assuming you've completed the necessary training and have all the special tools that are required, how long does it take to *change* a pair of shoelaces?

Question #3. I realize that shoelaces are quite expensive and may require a certain amount of financial planning. So the question is, how much money must you save in order to purchase a new set of shoelaces? (Let's figure the cost of *brand new* shoelaces, as opposed to the *previously owned* variety that are much more affordable.)

The point here, *Whiz-bang*, is that a bright, ambitious person like yourself would never in your life, logically, have ended up with a broken shoelace, much less two or three of them, if it wasn't for one simple reason. Me! It was *my* voice in your head that kept telling you that your fraying shoelace would last for, "One last tie. One last tie. One last tie." Then, on that day when you were running *stressfully* behind schedule, SNAP!

I am the cause of all procrastination. It pays me back with pro-activity and time to spare. As you will learn, I cause a lot more than just procrastination and snapping shoelaces. I created things like the fear of failure, which stops people from trying.

I also created *age* barriers. Like the thought of being too old before your time, which will stop you from starting certain new activities, or cause you to quit doing other activities long before you should have. The more of your youth I can take away, the younger *my* spirit remains.

By the time I have finished telling my secrets you will have learned more about artificial age barriers and other mental absurdities than you have ever imagined. As you will learn, I will make humans think whatever they have to in an effort to stop them from achieving their ultimate successes. But hey, don't take any of this too personally. Like the sign says, "Billions and Billions served."

Insecurity In a Can

When you were created it was intended that you become confident and strong, and make good use of all that you were given. *Every human is born with the power to achieve the impossible.* If you don't believe this, check your history. Throughout time you will find human after human who has proven this to be true. A couple of things that can help you achieve such lofty goals is the support and encouragement of the people around you. So if you decide to try something exceptional, like actually marketing one of those great new ideas of yours, I will make sure you get as little support as possible. This lack of support runs at a more profound level than you might think. For example, let's give you an active role in this very real story.

You are driving home from work and make a quick stop for a gallon of milk. Needing only a single item, you walk quickly through the grocery store, making your way to the cooler section.

With milk in hand you reverse your course and head for the checkout. Though your intent was to be swift, you manage to arrive at the checkout with your arms bear-hugged around your gallon of milk and twenty-two other items!

Now in line, there you stand, the fifth person in the row with four full carts ahead of you. The minutes pass. You're doing your best to balance the load, but with a "clank" a can of soup falls to the floor.

"Let me get that for you," says a man from the line next to yours.

"What a nice man," you think to yourself as the kind stranger bends down to fetch your now-dented soup can.

Eventually having made it through the line, you find yourself driving home along a poorly lit, rain covered road.

Just a few miles further, it's time to make a lane change. You lean forward looking into the rear view mirror on your driver's door, carefully ensuring there is plenty of room between you and the car behind you on the left. You click on the turn signal and YIKES! Here comes the other car! Like a speeding locomotive the other driver wildly accelerates to move up and block your lane change!

That's when you realize that the other driver, now flipping you a hand-gesture, is the same soup-fetching nice man from the grocery store.

After the shock wears off, you wonder if maybe you should have let him keep the soup! (But then again, I don't care much for chicken noodle.)

The point is, that I have made the people around you so insecure about your becoming successful, of you getting ahead of them at *anything*, that your getting ahead of them even in *traffic*, will make them do anything to cut off your plans. And by the way, thanks to you folks in Boston, Massachusetts. Your help in this area really helps my P & L statement. If you think I'm kidding, go drive in some traffic and play with your turn signal.

Here's a tip. The next time another driver tries to make a lane change, try a little experiment. Back off the gas and wave them in. You will feel better, stronger, and more successful for doing it. These are all key attributes on the road to fortunes.

The
Lawnmower Millions

Thanks to me, most of you believe that making large amounts of money is difficult, complicated, and requires a large amount of money just to get started. "It takes money to make money." Right?

The reality is, making large amounts of money isn't always complicated and doesn't always require a lot of money up front. Just to prove a point, I will tell you how to make a fortune. Not only that, I will also tell you how to do it without having to invest a lot of money, or brainpower. But keep in mind that after I do this, and I am going to, none of those excuses you've been using will have any merit. None of them! I should know, because I created them. I also made you *believe* them. So if you decide to finish reading this chapter, just remember this: Five years from now if you're not financially independent, it's *your* fault, not mine! So let's get on with it.

Welcome to what I call the "Lawnmower Millions." It's a very simple concept that is based upon *multiplying your efforts through other people*. Whether you choose to engage this principle exactly as it is written, or apply the same principle to something similar, the mathematics are the same. It works like this.

Next Saturday, take your lawnmower and mow your neighbor's lawn for $20.00. (Ask them first.) Do a good job so they'll have you mow it again. That's called *repeat business*. As long as you have the lawnmower running, ask another neighbor if you can mow their lawn also. That's $40.00. Plus, you can *write off* the cost of the gas you're using. Keep doing a good job and ask a couple more neighbors for *their* business. That's four lawns for a total $80.00.

At this point you are still financially *dependent,* relying on your own labor. And yes, I realize that mowing lawns is not sounding too glamorous, but who do you think is putting those thoughts in your head?

Now, get four more lawns for another $20.00 each. Then *duplicate,* or *multiply* your efforts, by asking one of the neighbor kids if they would like to become an *independent contractor,* and mow these four additional lawns for *$15.00* each. That's $15.00 for them and *$5.00* for you (from the $20.00 from each lawn). Get it? That means that while you are mowing back and fourth across one lawn earning your first $20.00, the neighbor kid is mowing back and fourth across a different lawn, earning you an additional $5.00, during the same frame of time.

Let's add this up. When you have finished your four lawns, you will have earned $80.00 from those four, and another $5.00 from each of the four lawns the neighbor kid mows, for another $20.00. This makes $80.00 + $20.00 for a total of $100.00.

Key point. That's $100.00 *in the same amount of time* it was taking you to make $80.00. That's a 25% raise. *When was the last time you received a 25% raise from the employer you are currently working for?*

Now, *duplicate* your efforts again by getting *four more* lawns and another neighbor kid (independent contractor). Now you will take in $80.00 from your four lawns, plus $20.00 from the first kid, plus another $20.00 from the second kid. That's $80.00 + $20.00 + $20.00 = $120.00, in the same amount of time it was taking you to make your original $80.00!

Are you getting the picture here? Keep in mind that each of the neighbor kids is taking in $60.00 for their efforts. They're happy because they are making money, and you're happy because you are making money.

Stay with me here.

Get four more lawns and another neighbor kid. Now, you will make $80.00 from your four lawns, plus $20.00 from the first kid, $20.00 from the second kid, plus $20.00 from the third kid. That's $80.00 + $20.00 + $20.00 + $20.00 = $140.00.

It's when you get the next four lawns that this gets real interesting. With four more lawns you'll make (hang in there) $80.00 from your four lawns, plus $20.00 + $20.00 + $20.00 + $20.00 = $160.00, in the *same amount of time* it was taking you to make your original $80.00. That's a 100% increase in pay. Or, if you choose, now you can do *absolutely nothing* on your Saturdays and still make $80.00 from the efforts of your independent contractors.

They mow lawns while you play golf, and you take in $80.00 dollars while you are playing. You have just become financially *independent* thanks to the process of, "duplication."

So get a fifth kid (independent contractor), and four more lawns. That will bring in $100.00 per Saturday. But why limit yourself to Saturdays? Why not Monday through Saturday? That brings in $600.00 per week. But why stop there? Why not keep growing? Instead of *five* contractors bringing in $600.00 per week, why not *fifty* contractors bringing in $6,000.00 per week? And so on, and so on, and so on. But if you don't like the idea of mowing lawns, you can apply this same principle to just about anything.

As you can tell, none of this is rocket science. Which is why you don't have to be a rocket scientist to make the big chips.

P.S. Isn't it ironic that grass is *green*?

Jimmy Hendrix

vs.

The Theory Of Evolution

Whether you are mowing lawns, building computers or racing automobiles, just how rich either one of us will become depends on how much of your potential you put to use, versus how much I can stop you from using. To understand how much potential that is, you must first understand how much potential you have. To do that, you have to take a spiritual look around you.

Consider the fact that you live on a huge planet. It's a planet that orbits around within an even larger universe. An impressive project by anyone's set of standards. The human mind and body, all the animals, all of the oceans and flowers and trees, are just as impressive, don't you think? So if you haven't figured it out by now, you need to accept the fact that something out there created all of this. Depending on where you live or what you believe, you may have different names for this "Creator," but he's out there just the same. As a matter of fact, before you finish the last chapter of this thing, I am going to knock you out of your chair by actually *proving* the existence of a divine Creator.

Call him what you will. Believe whatever you choose. But the same Creator who made the universe, also created humans. *And when he did, he gave every one of you special gifts and talents that you are supposed to be using.* Take for example the guitar players Jimmy Hendrix and Stevie Ray

14

Vaughan. Where do you think that kind of talent comes from? Yes, they lived hard lives on earth. They lived *short* lives on earth. But they made good use of their talents while they were *here* on earth.

Back when I lived on earth we went to church every Sunday. Even so, the preacher never said much about any "gifts" that we were supposed to be using. When one of us felt enthusiastic about trying something extraordinary, we never acted on it because we didn't understand how much we were *supposed* to be acting on it. **We never knew that *enthusiasm* was a gift that marked the path to our highest levels of achievement.**

Eventually, one by one, the Creator started taking away the gifts, and began giving them to humans who would use them. That may not seem fair, but it's no different than when a parent gives a child a special gift at Christmas, only to see that the child never uses it. After the gift is ignored long enough, the parent becomes sorry they gave the gift, and then takes it away and gives it to someone who will use and enjoy it. It is the same way in the spirit world. Like humans were saying back in the 1970's, "Use it or lose it."

While we're on the subject of creation, let's talk a little about that "evolution" bit that some of you have bought into. It's a good bit, and it keeps a lot of you off track. But the fact of the matter is that the body you are living in, the computer that is on your desk and the car in your garage did not evolve from the fungus on a cold piece of rock! Look, I only started that evolution thing because I was being opportunistic. A bunch of preacher-types started waiving their arms around and yelling things like, "Don't this! Don't that! Don't! Don't! Don't!" pointing their fingers and judging everybody and such. I didn't make the preachers do what they were doing, they just started doing it on their own!

If they had stopped long enough to actually *read* one of the books they were waiving, they would have known better. Nonetheless, a bunch of humans got *real* tired of being told negative and judgmental things and started looking for something else. So, payola! I just created something quick and easy that sounded good and called it, "Evolution." The rest as they say, is history.

That obviously puts you non-evolution Christian-types a cut above the rest!

Yep. Besides, **if man had evolved from apes, apes would not still be producing apes!**

Now do us both a favor and gather up all those books that made you the expert. You know the ones. The books on religion and spirituality that you, *yourself,* have carefully read cover to cover. The various editions of your chosen Bible that are filled with dog-eared pages, highlighter markings, index notes and torn binders. Go ahead. Get the *entire stack* of them.

Truth hurts, doesn't it?

Who do you think created those statements you keep hearing about scriptures and bibles having *too many interpretations,* or too many *historical and political changes* to have them be considered valid? Here's a hint. I did.

With books like the New Testament producing more millionaires than anything ever written, I had to do something to stop you from reading them. So I created some misinformation to do just that, and it worked.

You really should start reading. You might *"lern"* something.

Amen. Or should I say, A-fortune.

Uncle Bob's Cabin

My little place at the lake. The rustic old sign over the gravel driveway reads, "La La Land." With its sandy beaches and crystal clear water, some people love it so much they never leave. In fact, my little cabin at the lake has become the #1 fairy tale vacation paradise where both people and corporations allow their time and potential to peacefully slip away.

At Uncle Bob's cabin, trying something new, working a little harder or taking a bit of a risk, just seems *bothersome*. As a result, otherwise ambitious people and corporations become stuck in ruts, resting on their laurels and thinking they will somehow, perhaps *magically*, retain their assets and market share without rising up to the reality that surrounds them.

Good plan.

By the way, the hardware store is selling "Going Out of Business" signs for $3.00 each. And if these people don't leave the cabin soon, $3.00 is about all they'll have left. These types don't need "thinking out of the box." They need to get outside the four walls of the cabin, face reality and get back to work.

Who would have ever thought that my little absurdity of wealth without hard work would ever be taken so seriously by so many people!

Nonetheless, millions of humans just sit there waiting and even *expecting* someone to just hand them a *pot of gold*. The "Magic Million." I can't believe how many humans have bought into that! Apparently they enjoy spending time at the lake even more than I had expected. But when you think about it, why get caught up in working hard and *making* things happen when you can bathe in fairy tale riches with no effort at all!

Some humans actually believe they have *found* the Magic Million! This delusion apparently makes them believe that becoming arrogant and holding their nose in the air is not only appropriate, but somehow makes them appear more successful to other humans. "Let's see, if I act like a jerk other humans will think I am rich." Since most rich and successful people usually don't act that way, I am not sure I understand this completely. But if some of you want to act snooty over imaginary achievements that are not real to the rest of your planet, I guess it's okay with me. You can act any way you want to as long as you continue failing to achieve anything that matters.

Other humans come up to the cabin believing they can lose weight without changing their eating and exercise habits, or become great students without having to study, or become great athletes without having to train. Make no mistake, I enjoy having humans come to the lake for there is no better place for them to waste their precious time.

For example, let's use the achievement of a black belt in karate. While you are staying at the cabin, one option is to simply walk around thinking you *have* a black belt. Heck, you can even go to the corner store and buy one! But the fact of the matter is, if you ever needed to *apply the skill* of a black belt, you would end up with a black eye, instead.

Here's a painful piece of reality. While nobody can stop you from going out and *buying* a black belt, the possession of a black belt's skill can only be developed through a tremendous amount of *hard work*. Hour after hour, week after week, year after year. Training in Florida when you are too hot. Training in Minnesota when you're too cold. Training when you're too tired, or in pain. Taking your lumps. Taking your bruises. Getting up after being knocked down and continuing on. Eventually, and only after enough blood, sweat and tears have been shed will you ever be awarded your black belt. No delusions. No magic.

Outside of athletics the lessons remain the same. Suppose you want to grow a beautiful garden. The first thing you will need to do, is to have a load of black dirt delivered to your driveway. Next, you will have to go outside and place three items next to the dirt pile. A wheelbarrow, a shovel, and a lawn chair.

Now, if you were at the cabin, I would convince you to sit in the lawn chair, close your eyes, and listen to the following words:

"*Imagine* the garden."

"*See* the garden."

"It is a *lovely* garden, isn't it?"

Then you open your eyes. Hey! How about that! No garden! (I love that bit.) But here is a reality check. You can sit in a chair with your eyes closed for as long as you want to, but in the end there is only one way to make your garden. *You will eventually have to get up out of your chair and pick up the shovel.* Then, one shovel full at a time, you will have to fill the wheelbarrow. When the wheelbarrow is full, you will lift up on the heavy wooden handles and begin pushing the wheelbarrow across the soft grass of your lawn. When you reach the back yard, you have to dump the dirt and then push the wheelbarrow back to the driveway. Then, one shovel full at a time, you will have to repeat the process over and over again. Even though it may be a very warm and sweaty day, you will keep right on going. You will eventually plant the seeds for your flowers, water them regularly, and hope for sunshine. This is how you grow your garden. This is the real world, not La La Land.

Oh by the way, the next time you see someone walking around acting like they have achieved the Magic Million, don't worry. The Magic Million is sitting right here with me. But, as soon as you get to work bringing your dreams to life, I just might turn it into the *real* million, and let you keep it!

Big Profits From Big Kids!

Whether it's making contributions to a savings account or developing a person's athletic abilities, the principle is the same, "Get them started early." The same holds true with maneuvering people away from their assets. Take for example, a person's *intellect*. The sooner I get a person moving away from their intellect, the more *unused* intellect there will be for me to take away. For example, when I find a kid that's big for his age and turn him into a "Bully." Oh sure, there are better things for him to be doing with his mind and body than pushing around smaller kids, but in the long run it doesn't work to my benefit. After all, these are the formative years.

The Bully campaign became so successful that by the 1960's, Bullies began appearing in television shows and cartoon strips. Like, "Lumpy" who picked on Beaver. And who could ever forget those Charles Atlas cartoon-type advertisements where a skinny little guy at the beach would get sand thrown in his face by the local bully. The skinny little guy would then go away, lift a bunch of weights, and then return to the beach to throw sand back at the bully!

Consider the big picture. Do you really believe humans were created to wake up in the morning and say to themselves, "Let's see, I think I'll go to the beach, lift some weights and then throw sand in the face of a total stranger... yea, that's the ticket." What would be the point? There isn't one. It doesn't take any brains, either.

Not too long ago there was a gym class wrestling match. It was a heavyweight match between the school's biggest bully, "Big Jim," and a quiet kid named "Reed." Reed was chubby, pale, wore thick glasses and played the French horn in band class. *True* story.

What a mismatch! Everybody *knew* the wrestling match would be over in thirty seconds, and it was. It just didn't turn out as everyone had thought. The chubby French horn player had Big Jim down and on his back in seconds, and pinned inside of a half minute! The entire gym class, all sitting around the wrestling mat in their white t-shirts and school issue blue gym shorts, sat there with stunned looks on their faces. What they had never realized was that Big Jim, like most Bullies, spent most of his time thinking he was better and tougher than other kids just by virtue of his size. On the other hand, Reed, although he didn't look it, was actually quicker, stronger, tougher and most importantly, *smarter* than Big Jim. He knew more about wrestling than anyone realized. **His *knowledge* and his *will to win* had made him more powerful than anyone imagined.**

You can't judge a book by its cover, and you can't tell just by a person's appearance, including your own, those of you who will live to become famous authors, millionaire business people, or even become the toughest kid in school. History will testify that you all have the mental capability. But thanks to me, humans tend to forget that it is the mind and spirit that propels them toward the achievement of the impossible. The body working alone is far more limited.

Looking back on it, I should have never started the Bully thing. It has caused a bad reputation for a lot of young people who just happened to grow a little big for their age. But there wasn't much of a choice with the sand throwing bit. I tried reversing the roles and having the 98-pounders throw sand at the 200-pound high school jocks. The poor little guys seem to enjoy throwing the sand just fine, but they were getting themselves CLOCKED into the next time zone. That's when I decided to switch the roles back to

22

the way they were. After all, I was never interested in causing any physical harm. It's your minds that I like to play with.

P.S. Give me your lunch money, or else!

Robert Bakke

Air Bullets

You have probably never heard the term, "Air Bullets," so let me tell you what they are. Air bullets are *negative words*. Negative words like, dumb, fat, slow, idiot, impossible, crazy, never, moron, etc. Humans use negative words quite regularly but have never understood where they come from or the destructive power they carry. For example, suppose you tell someone that you want to become a professional football player. I'll counter, and have other people tell you that, "You will never make it because you're too small." After you hear this enough times, you will begin to believe it and give up.

Perhaps you are hoping to attend an Ivy League university. In that case, I will have people tell you, "That's impossible because you're not smart enough." If you hear this enough times, you will believe this also.

I will have people tell you just about anything if it will help to prevent the kind of super-achievement that you know, deep down, you are capable of. But don't worry. In the mean time, you can enjoy some time at Uncle Bob's cabin, where anybody can play football... at Yale!

Be careful not to underestimate the power of air bullets. They are considerably more destructive than the physical bullets that you are currently so concerned about. Physical bullets, which I play no part in, are fired from a gun and cause physical damage and even death, to the physical body. At this point the damage stops. **Air bullets, *negative words*, are fired from your mouth and cause damage to the *human spirit*, which lives forever.** So when a human spirit is damaged, the damage carries on into the next life where it must undergo repair. This is what makes air bullets so incredibly powerful, and why in the next life, humans (including yourself) are judged for every word you have spoken while here on earth. In the old days this was referred to this as, "reaping what you sow." Today, I just refer to it as *good comedy*, and here's why. When someone calls you something negative like, "stupid," a small amount of *their* intellect is taken away. When they call *another* person stupid, *more* of their intellect is taken away. So basically, when a human speaks negative words about someone else, they *themselves* slowly become that which they are saying about others! Like I said, you can call it whatever you want to, but I prefer to call it, "good comedy." But hey, it's not *my* problem.

My problems come from those of you who speak *positive* words. *Positive* words tend to cause people to become actively involved in life. They start setting goals. Then some of them start *achieving* goals. They become happier humans, and begin feeling more successful. **All of this causes learning to occur, which ultimately makes humans more powerful.**

Unlike negative words, *positive* words have the ability to elevate the human spirit to its highest possible potential. But this is nothing new. Dog trainers (which should actually be referred to as underpaid human trainers) have long been aware of this. They do a terrific job of teaching dog owners that their dogs will learn faster, perform better and live a happier life through encouragement and praise, as opposed to discouragement and criticism. This kind of teaching is allowed between a human and a pet, but would never be allowed between two humans. In fact, the only reason I allow it to continue between humans and dogs is because I happen to be a dog lover!

The ironic part of this is that humans have never figured out that dogs can teach humans more about how to treat other humans, than humans can teach themselves about how to treat other humans.

Large Waist, Large Wallet

Try as I do to bring humans down, it doesn't always work. In the interest of good sportsmanship it's only fair to tell you an occasional story about some of *your* victories and *my* failures. Like the failure I had when I tangled with a tenacious kid named, "Dan."

Talk about not judging a book by its cover, you might find it interesting that at the age of thirteen Dan was tipping the scales at nearly *three hundred* pounds. Another interesting detail is the fact Dan became a self-made millionaire at a *very* early age. Oh sure, *now* you're interested. So on with the story of the one we called, "Fat Albert."

Dan was not a typical little human, and not only because of his size. He was unusually quiet, and spent most of his time alone and indoors. Because he rarely went outdoors, his skin was unusually pale.

On a typical Saturday when other kids were outside throwing footballs and trading baseball cards, Dan was working alone in the small electronics workshop he had created in the basement of his parent's house.

His workshop was an interesting place. It was filled with televisions, radios, toasters, power tools, and other electrically powered gadgets, all in various stages of disassembly or repair. There were drawers filled with spare parts, repair manuals and test equipment, all neatly organized on a workbench.

Then there was Dan's bicycle. A red bicycle fairly similar to most, except for the two giant metal *trashcans* mounted on either side. Dan would ride his bike to nearby electronic repair shops looking for discarded electronic items. These scrapped items, often found in dumpsters, Dan would pile into his trashcan saddlebags and pedal home!

Are you picturing this? What a perfect opportunity to rally the other little humans and bombard Dan with air bullets. Which we did all summer, and all winter too.

When winter arrived Dan would put away his bicycle in exchange for a toboggan. He would pull his toboggan through the snow to the local dump, where he would load the toboggan full of scrap televisions and the like. He would then pull the heavily loaded toboggan, the frozen vapor of his breath rising out from the front of his fur trimmed hood, step by step, all the way home through the knee deep snow. Day after day he'd hear the other kids yelling, "What kind of junk did you find today, FAT ALBERT!"

Most little humans would have just stayed indoors. But not Dan, and for a couple of reasons. First of all, because Dan was too busy working on televisions to actually be *watching* them, he had no idea who Fat Albert was! So the fact that Fat Albert was a big, fat, teenaged cartoon character, didn't bother him.

Secondly, Dan's *knowledge* and *skill* had reached a point where he wasn't just taking televisions apart anymore. His knowledge had developed to where he was now actually *repairing* them. The other kids never knew it, but Dan could *smell* the money, and was not going to be denied. The following spring when his bicycle hit the road again, instead of just pedaling *home* with electronic scraps, he was also pedaling away with fully operational electronic products. Trashcans full! Televisions, radios, everything! Dan had taken scrap items home for *free*, repaired them with the spare parts he had collected over the years, and was now *selling* the items back to the very people who had thrown them away! *Pure profit!*

28

Dan, while still only a teenager, had developed his small electronics workshop into a fully functioning electronics repair station, complete with the latest test equipment. Test equipment he paid for with his own, *hard earned* money.

The news of his shop and the quality of his work began spreading quickly. It didn't take long before the shop had outgrown its basement location, and had to be moved into a single car garage.

But even the garage wouldn't be big enough for very long.

There was a town nearby located in a river valley. Because of its unusual location, the residents of the town were constantly struggling with poor television reception. Eventually, the homeowners of one particular neighborhood got together and bought a large television antenna for all their houses to share. This was a great idea, except for the fact it didn't work.

One at a time the local T.V. wizards would arrive, each promising to bring this one small neighborhood the reception they had hoped for.

One at a time, they all failed.

Finally someone asked, "How about calling that fat kid from across the river?"

And so Dan arrived. He didn't say much. He just stood quietly looking up at the antenna. Then he looked at the houses. He scratched his chin. That's when the quiet kid from across the river had a vision. It was a vision like those of all great leaders of achievement. Dan had begun thinking beyond just one small antenna and the houses of this one neighborhood. He began looking at all of the other houses. All of the buildings, the businesses, the challenging terrain, the people, the quality of life, the spirit of the community and the *creation of jobs.* This was not a "problem" for a single neighborhood. It was an opportunity to enrichen an entire town!

"Cable it."

Fat Albert had spoken, and so it would be.

The town had never had a cable television system, and Dan had never built one. But that had never stopped him before. It didn't take long before the entire town was enjoying better television reception and more television channels than they had ever imagined, and Dan was making *more money* than *he* had ever imagined. Why? Because Dan didn't just *build* the cable system, he *owned* it. Now, month after month, the checks from all of his cable subscribers were rolling in. Then Dan decided to duplicate his efforts, and began building more cable systems. Then he built *more* cable systems, and had more and more subscribers. More and more checks! Thousands of them! Month after month, the checks kept coming. Then he expanded into new areas. He began *designing* cable systems for other companies, and began *rebuilding* older cable systems for yet other companies. And still, month after month, all those checks just kept rolling in.

A small empire had been created.

To hear Dan tell it, he was successful because of his intensive knowledge of electronics, a strong work ethic, and because he had "remained free from the influences, barriers and limitations that bind people to mediocrity."

You should know by now where *influences*, *barriers*, and "limitations" come from. That's right, from me. I'm like a big, charging bull doing everything possible to knock you off your chosen path. Unfortunately, when I went charging at Dan... I missed.

"Ole'!"

Chat@walls.com

Have you ever listened to a marathon runner after the end of a race? They walk around saying things like, "I hit the first wall at eight." Or, "I hit the wall at twenty-three." In referring to the "wall" they are referring to intense moments of fatigue. Moments when their bodies had become so incredibly exhausted that taking another step seemed physically impossible. Yet they knew that if they were going to finish the race, they would have to be determined enough to take that next step. Then another, and another. Whatever it would take to penetrate the wall and finish the race. I didn't invent the walls, I just happen to discover that when a human hits one of them, it's a good time to have a chat. If you have run a marathon, you have heard my voice. It was the voice that kept mentioning the "Q" word. Or perhaps you've heard me whispering the words, "That's good enough." Like I did to the running back in the open field who slowed up on the 8-yard line thinking he had the touchdown, but ended up being caught and tackled from behind. Or the boxer who set out to spar ten rounds but quit after nine. Or the runner who started out on a ten mile tune-up, but took a short cut and made it home after just six and a half. All three of them were in active pursuit of their goal. All three heard the words, "That's good enough," and all three failed. The running back didn't score any points, the boxer got knocked out in his next bout, and when the runner tried to make her kick at the end of the race, it wasn't there.

I guess you could say I scored seven points, one knockout, and a First Place ribbon! Not too bad for a single day's work...

Do you know what these people are? Good listeners!

But not everyone is. For example, if you have finished a marathon, you are a poor listener. If you have actually won a marathon, you are a worse listener!

Nonetheless, after seeing how effective walls can be at causing people to give up at things, I decided to build a few of my own. For example, I built some walls into relationships, others into businesses, and even put some into schools, particularly colleges.

If you set a big goal and then make the decision to go after it, you better be seriously committed to that decision. If you aren't, you'll end up like so many humans who think that running in a marathon "sounds like fun." And for the first few miles it might be. But then they hit the wall. Do you know what happens to humans who enter marathons, or go to school, to have fun? When the going gets tough, they can't take it. They give up. They quit, and get "weeded out."

For those of you who haven't gone to college, weed-out classes are something I planted into the college system in an effort to get students to drop out of school. Students giving up on their professional careers can make me a fortune over the course of their lifetime. Weed-out classes work very well in this regard. They go something like this:

It is the first day of the new quarter. You have just spent your last fifty-cents on a video game and now you're late. You run three blocks to class (dropping a few papers on the sidewalk along the way), hoping you will be able to find the classroom without making too many wrong turns.

There, you see it, and slow to a jog as you pass through the classroom door. Sixty-two new faces all staring at you, thanks to the sound of your shoes pounding the floor as you covered the last seventy-five feet of hallway. Well that, and the fact that your wind blown hair now looks like something from the "There's something about Mary" movie.

Heading for the last empty desk (front row, of course), you sit down and spend the next forty-five minutes trying to look interested in what the instructor is teaching.

As the end of the hour approaches the instructor lists what appears to be the homework assignments for the entire quarter. You spend a few minutes writing them down and then begin thinking about the Monday Night Football game on ABC.

Then it happens. You hear the words, "Have this done by tomorrow."

You go into shock as you review the assignment list. "Read chapters one through five. Complete workbook assignments one through four. Quiz on chapter five. Outline for term paper." You go into a panic, and then waste the next few hours of precious time complaining about the assignment to some of the other students. With no more quarters in the pockets of your relaxed fit Levis, you abandon the video games and eventually return home.

The time has come to crack open your books and get started on your assignments.

A short time later, your roommate returns home with a pizza in hand, and heads for the television to watch the football game that you are undoubtedly going to miss.

A few hours later you hear the television click off and your roommate heads for bed.

Morning arrives. Having fallen asleep at the table, your roommate awakens you with barely enough time to finish your last assignment. Later that morning you turn in your work, only to find the entire process begins all over again.

Soon the days begin feeling like years. You can hardly find time for your other classes, much less your friends. Your hair is getting so dirty your scalp itches and if you're a guy, people start asking if you are growing a beard. Then something else happens. You begin wondering if it's all really worth it.

You've hit the wall, and that's when you're mine.

The moment you hit the wall is the very moment that every student, every athlete, every businessman, has to ask themselves how much they want what they are going after. If they want it bad enough, if *you* want it bad enough, you will have to find a way to finish. It's my job to see that you don't.

The famous Indy 500 race car driver Mario Andretti put it best when he said, "Before you can finish first, you first must finish."

A fairly profound statement for an open-wheel driver, but then again, I'm a NASCAR fan.

Your Brain In a Box

In 1997 there was a public speaker giving a presentation at the Neil Armstrong Elementary School in Cottage Grove, Minnesota.

The speaker was urging the students at the school to always keep an open mind, *and remember that the impossibilities of yesterday are the every day occurrences of today.*

One example he gave involved a letter that was written in the year 1829. It was written by the (then) Governor of New York, Martin Van Buren, and addressed to the President of the United States.

In his letter, Governor Van Buren expressed his concerns over the dangers of a new form of transportation known as, "Railroads."

He believed that the 15 m.p.h. speeds being reached by the railroad trains was "endangering the life and limb of the passengers!" He went on to tell the President, "Certainly the Almighty never intended for humans to travel at such *breakneck* speeds."

Today, little humans pedal their bicycles faster than that! You also have space shuttles that travel at 18,000 m.p.h. while upside down and backwards!

The public speaker went on to explain that technology will develop to where human beings will be able to walk *straight through walls...* that walls will dematerialize as people approach them, and re-materialize after they have passed.

One little boy stood up and said that was *impossible*, arguing that walls are "solid."

I revel in the fact that so many of you probably agree with that little boy. Unfortunately, the public speaker was fairly accurate. Look back to when the first (physical) walls were created. First there was one wall. Then there was a second. And then a third, and finally a fourth. Then a fifth was laid over the top of them to form a roof.

No more living in caves!

The two men on the outside of the structure thought it worked great, except they couldn't *get in.* The two men on the *inside* thought it was terrible, because they couldn't "walk through the walls" and *get out!* So they cut a *hole* in one of the walls, and the first *door* was invented.

But there was a problem. The wind and rain came through the open hole. So, they took the piece they had cut from the wall and placed it in front of the hole. Problem solved. Except it was heavy and hard to lift and move. And so the first hinges were created, making the door easy to swing both open and closed. Problem solved again. But then no light could come in, so they cut a hole in the door itself. But then the bugs flew in. So they invented the *screen.* And then *glass.* Then door *locks.* Then doors that opened *automatically* when you stepped on a mat.

Now doors open automatically when your presence is sensed by an *electric eye.*

So too will the day come when doors just flat out *dematerialize* when you approach them and *re-materialize* after you are inside!

Let's put this in musical terms. Suppose you lived in the days before the ability to record music was invented. If you wanted to play a song on a trumpet and save it to play later, what you would do? Would you try playing the song and catching it in a shoebox? You could try, but you would have to be quick with the lid or the song would escape! A couple hours later, provided you did a good job of trapping, would the song still be in the shoebox?

Do you think this would work?

If it doesn't, you could try trapping the song in a piece of wood or something. Just blow the trumpet at the piece of wood and the wood should absorb the sound just fine, don't you think? But if that doesn't work, maybe you could try blowing the trumpet at a piece of plastic. Certainly *that* will work. Then later, try spinning the plastic real fast, and if you are lucky the sound will come out from centrifugal force!

If that doesn't work, maybe you can try placing a steel needle on the plastic, with a speaker connected to the needle, and if the needle can pick up the sound, maybe it will come out the speaker.

Are you catching on?

Let's keep going.

Trapping the song on plastic might work, but if the plastic gets scratched, those scratches might be picked up by the needle and send scratch noises through the speaker. If that happens, try blowing your trumpet at magnetic tape and trap the sound that way. If the steel needle doesn't work on magnetic tape, just design a flat faced magnetic head to gently rest on the tape. If the magnetic head resting on the tape causes a hissing sound, perhaps you can think of something else. Something that won't have to touch anything at all. Like a *laser beam.*

That's the ticket! A laser beam! Here's what you do. Figure out how to trap a song into a small round plastic disk. Then, pass the plastic disk through the light of the laser beam. Have the light of the beam, without actually touching the disk, lift the sound out of the disk. Then, send the sound to speakers across the room, with no physical wires actually attached to them, and have the sound come out of those speakers! (By the way, the original laser beams required a facility the size of a small warehouse. All you'll need to do is find one the size of your thumbnail.)

So what is my point? My point is, that at one time in history trapping sound, *recording* sound, on *anything*, was impossible! But through creativity and determination, humans eventually had created plastic records to play on record players, magnetic tape to play in cassette players, and CD's that are played through the laser beam of a compact disc player.

You may not have noticed it, but the *impossibilities* of yesterday have become the everyday occurrences of today. I have taught you to take this kind of thing for granted because it causes you to disregard the future potential of today's greatest ideas.

Doesn't it make you wonder, just a *little*, how far along you would be if I *wasn't* so good at my job? After all, fifteen miles per hour really isn't breakneck speed, and today there is a laser beam in every home. So do you really think it is impossible for a door to someday dematerialize?

You work on that. In the mean time, I have to put a gag in that speaker guy.

May The Force Be *Against* You

Read this:

$$3 + 3 = 6$$
$$3 - 3 = 0$$
$$3 \times 3 = 9$$

This is how easy it is to stifle large amounts of human development. As a matter of…

What?

You don't get it?

Okay, since the numbers are rather large, look at it this way.

Each math problem has a different answer!

Get it, now?

What! (No wonder you can't catch UFO's.)

Okay, let's break it down even farther. Each math problem has a *different* answer, but each math problem also has a *correct* answer. No one answer is any better or any worse than the other. They are all *equally important*. The goal of addition is to add 3 + 3 and come up with 6. The goal of subtraction is to subtract 3 from 3 and come up with 0. And so on, with no arguing or disagreements over the level of their individual merit. They are all "free" to pursue and to achieve their individual goals.

If humans applied this same comfort level to differences among each other, there would be super-achievement occurring everywhere. This is why I had to go after your asset called, "Free Will."

Imagine the power of 1000 people all gathered in one auditorium. You would have 1000 different minds, 1000 different goals, 1000 different enthusiasms, 1000 different life experiences and more, right there in front of you. Imagine accepting each of their lives as *being correct for them*, just as *freely* as mathematics accepts that 3 x 3 = 9 is correct for multiplication. No judging, no arguing. You would have unlimited knowledge, expertise, thoughts, perspectives, philosophies and *respect*, all flowing freely. It would produce an environment capable of *unlimited* intellectual horsepower. But thanks to me, it will never happen.

Do you think I am kidding? Go ahead and put 1000 people in an auditorium. If I get my way, do you know what you will end up with? You will have some people judging what the other people are driving for automobiles. Others will be gossiping about the clothes someone else is wearing. You will find parents trying to redirect the goals of their children. Teachers will be trying to convince students that science class is more important than auto shop. Democrats will be fighting with Republicans. Christians will be judging non-Christians. Ski racers will be thinking they ski better than mogul skiers. Wrestlers will be thinking they are tougher than karate guys, on and on and on! Everyone will be trying to convince each other that *their way* is the way things ought to be. With that philosophy, 1000 people don't need 1000 minds. They only need one. Whose one mind do they use then, yours?

What's my point? It's this. There was an old man who lived in a neighborhood. Everywhere he went, whether it was raining or not, he always carried an open umbrella over his head. Because he did this, everyone said bad things about him. Some people even referred to him as, "dangerous." The neighborhood children were constantly warned to stay away from him.

Finally, on one rebellious Saturday afternoon, one of the children cautiously approached the crazy old man and asked why he always carries an open umbrella? The old man replied with a kindly smile, "*I am allergic to the sun.*"

Originally what had happened was, on a warm and sunny day someone witnessed the old man carrying an open umbrella. Not being open minded enough to consider that the old man may have a *reason* for carrying the umbrella, they simply, ignorantly, concluded that he was out of his mind. So that person told a friend, who in-turn told a friend, and so on. Before you knew it, the entire neighborhood believed he was nuts! But in reality, *they* were the ones acting mindlessly. Not one of them had taken the initiative to ask any questions of the old man. They lived in judgement and ignorance, and in doing so never enjoyed the friendship of a very kindly neighbor.

Everybody has the right to carry an umbrella, whether they are allergic to the sun, or not!

Originally, you were all created to be free to think what you wanted to think. To believe what you wanted to believe, and to follow the enthusiasm that *you* were given. By living this way, you begin to understand that it's okay if the person next to you lives a life that is different from your own. That they might have a reason for doing something the way they are doing it, even if there are ways of doing it differently. And that it's okay if someone puts on a coat, even if *you* are not cold.

By spending less time judging each other, you could spend more time asking questions and learning from each other, ultimately helping you with your own thinking and doing. With this type of intellectual cooperation, having 1000 people in the same room would create something more powerful than you can imagine. That is why taking away free will was so important. When I did, it stifled the intellectual development of millions, and the earth became less powerful.

A Hand In The Air

If You Dare

Consider this. I have made so many humans so judgmental, that many of you now actually *fear* being judged by your peers. You fear it so badly that the number one fear in the United States has become speaking before a group of other humans! (Fact.) Look it up!

When was the last time you raised your hand and asked a question while sitting among a group of strangers? Probably a while now, which is exactly how intellectual growth becomes stifled.

For instance, Mark is a professional pilot. A jet captain. While attending fight school to learn the systems of a new jet aircraft, the following situation occurred.

Mark and the other pilots were attending a class on the new aircraft's electrical system. As the instructor began drawing out and explaining the system, Mark became confused. A few minutes later he was completely lost. He wanted to raise his hand and have the instructor start over, but since the other pilots appeared to be following along with the instructor, Mark didn't want to appear "stupid" in front of the other pilots.

A few minutes later Mark couldn't tolerate being confused any longer, so he reluctantly raised his hand and asked the instructor to start over.

Do you know what happened? The very instant the instructor started over, the *entire class* picked up their pencils, sat forward in their desks and

43

focused intensely at what the instructor was explaining. In other words, Mark wasn't the only pilot who was confused. The *entire class* was confused! Every one of them, in total confusion and not learning one thing, all because they were individually afraid of raising their hand and being judged negatively by their peers.

Mark had the courage to raise his hand and the entire class became smarter! Think of this in terms of intellectual growth. Had Mark sat quietly, in fear of being judged, how much learning would have occurred?

None.

But Mark conquered his fear of being judged, and asked his question. When he did, *a higher level of learning occurred,* and in this case, even the skies became safer because of it! After the class several of the pilots came up to Mark and thanked him for being "the brave one."

Judging other people with your own set of perceptions stifles your own intellectual growth. Living in fear of *being judged by others* also stifles your intellectual growth. Only when humans stop judging each other and start *asking things* of each other will your knowledge base truly begin to expand. Only then can your intellectual engine become the unlimited thinking machine that it was intended to be. *And as you will learn later on, when it comes time to making money, your knowledge is ultimately what people pay you for.* So the person who opens their mind and *learns the most*, wins. But you better get going, because I am taking away everything you are not using, and it is making me smarter by the day.

You Can't Judge a Millionaire

By His Overalls

All of this talk about humans misjudging each other reminds me of another story. It's about a man from the small farm town of Platte, South Dakota. His name is Lowell.

Lowell is a simple man, whose idea of comfort was and still is, wearing an old faded blue pair of Osh Kosh B-Gosh overalls with no shirt underneath. Lowell is a God fearing man. A believer in spiritual things who unlike many religious sorts, actually *reads* his chosen Bible seven days a week.

After high school, Lowell completed a college education and then moved to a big city. It was just Lowell, a Bible, and his Osh Kosh B-Gosh overalls.

As the years passed, Lowell found himself with a good job, a loving wife, four kids (3 boys, 1 girl), and a mortgage payment. The American dream for many of you, but not for him. Lowell really didn't want to work for anybody. He wanted his own business.

After years of searching, Lowell believed he had finally found what he had been looking for. He and two friends made the decision to start their own sales organization, selling agricultural and industrial products, and related supplies. They were so serious about doing it that they *quit their jobs* to make it happen. A fairly gutsy move considering they barely had a spare

45

nickel between the three of them. As a matter of fact, spare cash was so tight that their first office, just like Fat Dan's, was set up in an old, unheated, single car garage.

At this point in the story, ask yourself a question. If Lowell lived in *your* neighborhood, what would you be thinking at this point? Would you be wishing him well? After all, he has a household to support, so wouldn't you be offering him support and encouragement? If you are the kind of decent human being you like to think you are, wouldn't you be wanting to see him succeed? Of course you would, but not Lowell's neighbors.

You should have heard them.

"Lowell has a family to feed, how could he be this selfish." Others were saying he had, "lost his mind." In fact, one of Lowell's relatives called Lowell's wife and actually offered to pay the cost for him to see a psychiatrist! Absolutely true! Friends, neighbors and relatives were attacking him from all sides! But what business of it was theirs? Besides, instead of spending their time and energy *judging* Lowell, they could have been offering to help him! *Perhaps they could have learned how they too could have become self-employed.* If Lowell's neighbors didn't want to help him, they could have at least wished him well, and then gone about pursuing their own goals. But they did neither. All they wanted to do was judge, criticize and hope he failed. Why? So he didn't succeed and in-turn, make *them* feel unsuccessful.

Lowell just kept marching straight ahead, working literally, around the clock. He would work at his office all day, and then with a hired work force of neighbor kids, assemble sales brochures and packets, late into the evening.

It didn't matter how much distraction and ridicule he was surrounded by. His faith in achieving the impossible would not buckle.

How can humans be so similar and yet so different?

As Lowell's business and the *hundreds of jobs he had created,* became more and more successful, his neighbor's voices turned from judgmental, to jealous. That's when they stopped talking to him altogether. Finally, in his fifth year in business and generating nearly 100-million in yearly sales, Lowell, still wearing his Osh Kosh B-Gosh overalls, built a mansion on a Minnesota lake and quietly moved his family away. Since that time Lowell has made it his mission to volunteer his time each week to helping others generate their own wealth, and each Friday, he leads a Bible study for prison inmates helping them to find a better path for themselves.

Lowell enjoys sharing his knowledge and helping others. He would have also enjoyed helping his former neighbors, but thanks to me they were in no mood to ask him for help.

This is a very true story, and one that marks my success with Lowell's neighbors, and my total failure with Lowell.

Lowell... such a poor listener.

As a matter of fact, if you live on a farm you almost certainly have some of his products on your shelves, in your equipment, and on your crops right now. The name of his company is...

Oh forget it. Lowell has cost me too much already. And if you follow his example of courage and determination, now you will too!

I'm sorry I opened my mouth.

Winning Isn't Everything

(*Losing* is where the money is...)

Let's say it like this:

"Hey, do you want to have some fun? Let's all get together and work *real* hard. Let's spend *hundreds* of hours practicing. We will all make *big* sacrifices, and if we're lucky, we will do poorly! We won't get a thing for our effort! Not even a small trophy! Come on, it will be great!"

Maybe we should put the business spin on this:

"Okay Nancy, here is what the board wants you to do. Throw the payroll budget out the window. Spend whatever overtime hours you need. Hire more people if you have to. We are expecting you to burn the midnight oil on this one. All of our jobs are on the line. We are all counting on you, Nancy, so remember, do poorly."

The fact of the matter is, that winning is undeniably important. *Doing well* is important. It is the only natural and fair conclusion to all of someone's hard work. Ambitious beings, whether they are human or not, don't dedicate themselves to big goals and then go through all of the hard work and sacrifice everything they do because they want to achieve average results! Ambitious beings set big goals and work hard because they want to *be the best*. We enjoy the *pursuit of excellence*.

48

It should be fairly easy for you to tell when I am playing with someone's mind in this regard. For example, when a parent tells a child that winning isn't everything, but at the same time, expects the child to get all A's on their report card. The next time someone tells you that winning, or achieving excellence, isn't important, just ask a question or two. For example, if they were going into the hospital for surgery, would they want an *average* surgeon, or the surgeon that is regarded as the *finest in the world?* Or when getting on an airliner, would they want a flight crew that is *below average* with a poor safety record, or would they prefer to have the pilots from Air Force One?

Some of my most successfully crafted misconceptions revolve around *excellence* and *winning*. What makes this so easy is the fact that every one of you must work so hard to achieve them. You can't simply purchase excellence in a store. Be that as it may, I continue to cause millions of you to spend *billions* of dollars each year, constantly searching for an easy way to win. Do you think I'm kidding? Okay. "Easy weight loss, physical fitness in 5-minutes and day, and Get Rich Quick!" I rest my case.

The reason it is so essential to prevent the understanding of excellence, is because the very process that you live through in developing excellence in one activity, is a process that transcends *all* activities. In other words, if you have successfully completed the process of excellence once, you can successfully complete it again at something else. That means the more things you get good at, the more things you will *know* you can get good at. At that point you will have captured *confidence*, which is one of the most powerful attitudes a human can possess.

Confidence and *excellence* are two very interesting and misunderstood attributes. For instance, excellence exists as a skill, and as such it has obvious limitations because it can *only be applied to the skill to which it applies.*

49

Think about it. Does being an excellent gymnast automatically make you an excellent water skier? Of course it doesn't. Just because you are good at one thing doesn't automatically make you good at something else.

While excellence is a skill, *confidence* is an attitude. It is a very deep state of mind that does not share the single-task limitations of excellence.

Confidence can be applied to anything. Although it should be pointed out that a human's confidence is most easily noticed when that human is performing in their area of expertise. For instance, a great gymnast is most noticeably confident while performing gymnastics. But what do you suppose happens when the gymnast decides to try something new?

Let's say you have your family's 325 horsepower Malibu ski boat for the weekend and decide to take a couple of friends out water skiing. One of them is a couch potato (because he's a good listener), the other is our gymnast.

You finally arrive at the lake and after backing down and pulling ahead, and backing down and pulling ahead three or four times on the boat landing, you finally manage to get the trailer into the water and launch the boat. It's a perfect day. Clear skies, warm temperatures and the lake is as flat as a mirror.

With the rumbling V8 warmed up and the ski rope untangled, you get your couch potato friend into the water. You give him a few pointers and tell him to yell, "HIT IT" when he's ready. After three or four unsuccessful attempts and a nose rammed full of lake water, Mr. Couch potato has hit the wall, and gives up.

Into the water goes the gymnast. After giving her the same instructions you hear the words, "HIT IT!"

You throttle up the power. One thousand one, one thousand two... and SPLASH! Down she goes, and so it goes a few more times until you ask her if she wants to quit for a while. Although she's breathing pretty hard and has swallowed about a gallon of lake water, she replies, "Just a couple more tries. I think I've almost got it." Sure enough, a couple more tries and she's up and skiing.

A little later in the day, after a rest and a bite to eat, you ask your friends if they want to make a second run. Your couch potato friend replies, "No thanks. I'll ride shotgun." Our gymnast on the other hand, says something to the effect of, "Sure!" Followed by something like, "Is it very difficult to drop one?" In other words, she wants to try skiing on one ski. Even though that means wiping out a few more times, you can bet she will finish the day skiing on a single ski.

Was she able to learn to ski because of gymnastics? Not necessarily. She learned to ski because of her *attitude*. **She believes in herself and her ability to achieve because of her accomplishments: her *excellence* and *winning* in gymnastics.** Don't forget that there was once a first day for gymnastics also, and many days that followed when she felt clumsy and awkward. But because she liked gymnastics so much she kept at it. She hung in there, and after years of hard work, those routines that once seemed impossible were eventually mastered. Having achieved excellence at something, in this case gymnastics, has helped to give her confidence in her ability to learn and achieve other things. In other words, she knows that if she's done it once, she can do it again at something else. **Certain fundamental principles of the process of achievement transcend all areas of achievement.** This entire process is no different than when a businessman or C.E.O. steps in to save a failing airline, and then later takes on the job of saving a failing convenience store chain, even though he or she had no previous experience in either of those specific industries. These kinds of achievements are possible because certain fundamental principles will remain the same.

That is why doing well, achieving excellence and winning, is so important. It builds confidence in knowing that you have what it takes, to do whatever it takes, to eventually succeed at what you are setting out to do. The more things you become good at, the more things you will *know* you can become good at. This is why I have tried so aggressively to disrupt your pursuit of excellence, particularly in the area of school athletic programs.

Unfortunately for you, young couch potatoes that never get up on their water skis, later become adult couch potatoes who never even *try* to get up on water skis! Some of these same couch potatoes become the adults in charge of deciding whether or not the athletic programs in your schools are worth keeping.

I enjoy helping these folks get into positions of authority, because good couch potatoes do not understand how winning in athletics develops winning attitudes towards other things, including math class, and later on in business.

Achieving excellence, whether it is at ice hockey, algebra, or flying airplanes, builds confidence. It is what helps you overcome the adversities, the frustrations and "the walls" that are lying in your path. For a spirit like myself, this can get *real* expensive. So when it comes time for working hard and achieving excellence I just have one thing to say...

"Have another *donut*." My treat!

One Second to Achieve Your Dreams

Getting humans hung up on their age has been a very successful campaign. It wasn't too long ago when most of you thought that reaching the age of 30 meant you were, "Over the hill." That was of course, until Jimmy Connors came along and refused to give up on playing tennis.

Are you reading this, *James?* What on earth were you thinking when you won at Wimbledon at the age of 30? Do you have any idea how much of my work you were undoing when you were still playing competitive tennis at the age of 39? Thanks to efforts like yours we now have professional football players still playing in their forties! Olympic records are now being set by athletes who are older than ever, and that's not all.

In January of 2001, hockey player Mario Lemieux at the age of 35, came out of a nearly four year retirement scoring two goals and five assists in his first two games!

On August 20, 2000, at the age of 50, professional golfer Tom Watson set a course record of 65 at Valhalla Golf Club.

In 1999, at the age of 52, Carlos Santana lit the Grammy Awards on fire winning *eight* Grammys!

Of all people, even Sonny Barger (the original Hell's Angel of the same named motorcycle gang) at the age of 61, became a published author.

Joe Paterno, Head Coach of the Penn State Nittany Lions football team, signed a contract extension at the age of 73!

Come on you guys, you're killing me here. Everywhere I look there are people in their sixties and seventies still water skiing and running marathons!

All the more reason I'm glad I am retiring.

Humans are realizing they can do more, and for much longer than ever before. Except of course, for those guys at the Airline Pilots Association. They are still forcing their best and most seasoned pilots to retire at the age of 60 (soon to be 63), but why should I care. I have never flown on an airplane (after my time). But *you* on the other hand…

The reality of human age is that while your body is limited to approximately 100-years of earth time, *your spirit lives on forever*. To put this in perspective, your 100-years of earth time goes by in about *1-second* as it relates to the eternal clock. That's right, *one second*.

One-thousand-one! Your life on earth is over.

When you look at your life on the one-second scale, that means that 10 of your human years are equal to about *one-tenth* of a second! 20-years, two tenths of one second. 60-years, six tenths of one second, and so on. When making an age comparison between two humans, if one of you is twenty years old and the other is forty years old, that makes you, as it relates to the eternal clock, about *two-tenths* of a second apart as you might measure it on a stop watch. This explains why so many of you say things like, "I don't *feel* twenty-nine." Or, "I don't *feel* fifty-two." Or, "I don't *feel* seventy six." That is of course, until I have someone tell you something like, "You know Bill, you are 44-years old now. When are you going to put those skis in the attic and start *acting your age*."

Have you ever noticed how the last several years have gone by in what seems like a *flash*?

54

Do you remember the last time you thought to yourself, "Where has the time gone?" Of course you do, because *one-second* goes by quickly, and that means your time on earth isn't as long as you might think.

We all realize that accumulating a number of injuries can eventually bring a halt to certain activities. But do you realize how many joys of life you have given up just because of the twelve insignificant pages of a *paper* calendar?

Just because there are thirty-one tiny boxes per page and some cute little puppy pictures doesn't mean a calendar is worth changing your life for, does it?

It hangs by a thumbtack for Pete's sake!

If the twelve pages of a paper calendar are making you feel old, turn it into twelve little paper airplanes and let the kids have it!

Successful humans are strong enough to *act their spirit.* They do not live by the absurdity of a calendar age. But if you want to keep giving up your passions, I will gladly keep collecting them. It is your life, so decide for yourself. But since you have less than *one-second*, I suggest you get moving!

Robert Bakke

The Peanut Butter Fitness Program
(Would you prefer Regular, or Chunky?)

After reading the last chapter you should be realizing that humans are more similar in age than you might have previously been thinking. When you consider the big picture it changes your perception of one another, doesn't it?

More on that later.

Part of the perception problem with age is the result of my carefully crafted plan to begin reducing your physical condition as early as possible. An obvious part of that plan was to have the people around you say what they could to talk you out of doing physically active things. This has been "hugely" successful (a sarcastic pun). It has caused many adults to think, deep down, that staying in shape, staying in real shape, is only for high school jocks and professional athletes. Do you know what else I did? I STOLE GYM CLASS! And when I did, I took the fun right out of work.

You may want to pay very careful attention to the following.

Most adults blame their lack of physical condition on their age. Is age really a part of the problem? Sure it is. But do you know the "bigger" problem? (Another pun there.) The bigger problem is, they have slowly forgotten about *gym class!* Think about it. As a child, you play all day. Then you go to grade school and have gym class every day. Then you attend junior high and high school, and do you know what you have there? Gym class! Every day! Where my plan starts taking "shape" (and yet another pun) is when you go off to college. In college you will be lucky to have gym class two days a

56

week at best, and then only for the semesters that it is required. After college you will go off to work, where finally, you will have no gym class at all! Worse than that, you will probably end up sitting *still* in a chair more than 40 hours each week!

To summarize, when you are a child you play *every day*. When you are an adult, you *don't*. It is that simple. Some of you manage to go off to health clubs after work, but the fact is, the overwhelming majority of you, don't.

Do you know what every business *needs* but that I have kept from providing? *Gym Class.* Physical fun!

Recess!

Wouldn't it be interesting if every working adult was provided a locker at work with a change of clothes and thirty minutes each day for mandatory *recess?* And don't think for an instant that I don't realize some of you think you're too old for such a child-like notion. Who do you think makes you think that way? But then again, maybe you are too old. After all, your age is pushing all of what, 4-tenths of a second?

You're right. That's *old*.

Most companies have a lawn where a volleyball net could be set up, or a warehouse where employees could use some floor space for aerobics, or a basketball hoop. Perhaps the company could provide a company sponsored health club membership for employees and their families. These ideas are not out of the question, but if you think they are, perhaps you need to come home from *the lake*.

This reminds me of a story. In earth years, Ted is a forty-two year old, highly educated, white-collar professional. One day at work, Ted was explaining to a forty-six year old "superior" how excited he was about his softball game from the night before. The "superior" responded with an annoyed look and said, "What's it like being a 19-year old boy trapped in a forty-two year old body?" Ted took the attempted putdown as his greatest compliment of the day. He then went water skiing after work and forgot all about it.

I have duped employers and employees alike into forgetting that the greatest mind in the world can only go as far as its body will allow it to. If you are an employer who expects exceptional performance from your employees, you had better start thinking about the enhanced fitness level of your employees. So give them a break, and let them have a little fun.

Regardless of what you have accomplished in the past or what you might think you are capable of in the future, your fitness level will play a vital role in your performance. And while there are a number of successful people who scoff at physical fitness, they are failing to realize that they could be *more* successful if they were in better physical condition. This is so easy to prove that I can do it using something as simple as a golf ball.

For a golf ball, the *opportunity for advancement* is generated by the impact of a golf club. When a golf ball in good physical condition is struck by a golf club (the opportunity for advancement) it responds by covering a very long distance. On the other hand, a golf ball in poor condition, when given the same *opportunity to advance*, responds poorly.

The most difficult obstacle in getting yourself into good physical shape is in the fact that it takes so much hard work.

Getting into good physical condition is difficult, but it pays big dividends. Have you ever noticed how many wealthy and successful people talk about how far they run every day? Turn on a talkshow. Read a magazine. You can't escape it. This is not to say that you can jog your way to fame and fortune, but it certainly doesn't hurt. Physical activity keeps your muscles in tone, burns off calories, reduces stress, and most importantly, brings fresh oxygen into your respiratory system, which I might add, you humans seem to pay very little attention to. This really isn't my area, but consider this. You can live without *food* for a very long time. Several weeks (but don't try it). You can live without *water* for several days (but don't try this either). *But you can only last about three minutes without air, and you're dead!* That's right, three short minutes and you and I have a tee time together.

If for no other reason, *regular exercise increases the supply of your most precious life force.* FRESH AIR!

Finally, if you put all of this together and add a few special ingredients, you come up with the Peanut Butter Fitness Program. Here it is:

Step 1. Although we haven't really talked about it, get plenty of sleep. Take a nap if you feel like it. The bottom line is, no rest, no energy. On the other hand, you can stay up all night and look like Freddie Krueger the next day. Your choice.

Step 2. Treat yourself to daily exercise to provide your body with muscle tone and plenty of fresh oxygen. This is the single most important thing you can do for yourself, and you will look and feel better because of it. Or, you can smoke cigarettes and I'll get us that tee time.

Step 3. Drink plenty of fresh water, it's what your body is essentially made of. If you don't like fresh water, you can drink beer. It's not as good for you, but it helps the stock portfolios of large size clothing makers.

Step 4. Finally, eat a balanced diet with some kind of fruit everyday. Then it's okay to have a little of this, a little of that, and even an occasional dessert for fun. Unless of course, you are one of those know-it-all humans who keeps running around scaring people about the food they are eating. In that case I just have two words for you. "Peanut Butter." That's right, peanut butter. Do you know why? Because 99% of the people who have contracted terrible diseases, have been turned down for prom or slipped on a banana peel, have all been linked to eating the same food. That's right, *peanut butter!*

And yet the FDA continues to allow it on store shelves. Hummmm...

Get a life! Now where's that jelly?

We Don't Need No *Stinking* Experts

Experts are people who have invested large amounts of time and sacrifice in an effort to achieve masterful levels in a specific area, and even though they don't always come up with the best possible advice or solutions, *legitimate* experts should be respected for the tools they have developed.

Since experts possess knowledge that can help other humans become successful, it is essential that I do what I can to interfere with their teachings.

Interfering with expert advice was more difficult than I expected, particularly with focused, *productive* humans.

Productive humans tend to be both *humble* and *confident*, which is a surprisingly tough combination to crack. They are humble enough to accept the fact that they *don't* know everything, which prompts them to seek the advice of an expert. They are also confident enough to believe that while they don't know everything, they do know *something*. This humble, yet confident approach causes them to seek out experts to *assist* them with their thinking, as opposed to other humans who use experts to actually *do* their thinking for them. This is an important difference. Because when I get you to shut down *your own thinking* in lieu of someone else's, you allow your mind to become idle and in turn, never take full advantage of your own intellectual capabilities.

We can use something like religion to clarify some of this. For example, there are millions of humans who consider themselves religious people.

Even though they get up and go to church every Sunday, many of them, *most* of them, have *never* taken the time to actually *read* their chosen Bible. Not *once* cover to cover. The reality of their religion is that they spend their time in church listening to the preacher, the *expert*, tell them what they *should* believe, but they never actually take the time to read and discover *for themselves* that which they *do* believe.

Doesn't it make sense that the preacher's efforts would be amplified if you also engaged your own intellectual engines?

Preachers are legitimate experts in their field, and when you add upon their expertise with your own mental horsepower, you will *both* learn more, as opposed to having one of you do all the thinking for the other.

Another way in which I interfere with expert advice is to get you to listen to people who really aren't experts at all. For example, here's one way that I might interfere with the advice of *motivational* experts. Consider the attitude they call, "Positive Thinking." The initial intent of positive thinking was a good one. It was intended to create focus and motivation energized by the deep belief in a triumphant outcome. But do you know what? By creating *bogus experts* I was able to turn positive thinking into positive *stinking*, and now it works something like this:

Cindy is attending college. Thursday nights are the big-time party nights at her school. Unfortunately for Cindy's party plans, she has a very important exam on Friday.

Thursday afternoon, Cindy's friends bring on major heat to get her to go out and party as opposed to staying home and studying for her exam. Cindy buckles. She lets her friends *do her thinking for her*, and she goes out partying.

Friday afternoon Cindy takes the exam. After finishing the exam she leaves the classroom and tells her friends that she "doesn't think it went very well." To this, her friends the *bogus experts* reply, "Think positive!"

Cindy's *expert* friends go on to convince her that she's only being *paranoid,* and that if she "thinks positive" everything will turn out okay. Cindy decides to agree with them, and goes out partying again.

Cindy should have been *considering the source* of the advice. Does she honestly believe her friends know the first thing about achievement psychology? Well, apparently she does.

Not only did I get Cindy to *let her friends do her thinking for her*, she actually believed that positive thinking *after* the exam would improve her grade!

"Positive Stinking" at its finest.

Once an exam has been taken, or a sales presentation has been given or a business proposal submitted, no amount of misguided, after-the-fact high hopes are going to change the result!

Achievement is built upon those things you do *before* you engage upon your mission. Understanding how to achieve your goals is no more difficult than this:

When you have a goal, you must align your behavior with that goal.

What that means is, if you want to be a professional athlete but you don't want to exercise, you won't get there. If you want to be a scientist but you don't want to study, you won't even make it to college. Get the point?

Let's say you have a dream. Your dream is to have a big new home on Lake Minnetonka (the Midwest's finest), a Wellcraft Scarab parked at your dock, two weeks of scuba diving in the Caymans every year and a Dodge Viper in the garage.

Sound good?

Now let's check that against reality. Let's say that you're still in school and surrounded by friends like Cindy's friends. The kind of friends who talk you into skipping school, or going out instead of studying. The kind of friends who offer *positive stinking* as the solution to your problems. Do you know why I have you listen to these types of *bogus experts?* It's because young humans who skip school later become adults who skip work. Adults who skip work get passed up for promotions. Promotions are where the money is, and houses on Lake Minnetonka cost money. Therefore, adults who skip work fail to achieve their dreams, which I in-turn collect like shot glasses.

What does all this mean for young humans? It means this. **Young humans who skip school become adult humans with no money!** And do you know what *that* means?

No Dodge Viper!

Think with your *own* brain! That's what it is there for.

Running The Mentathlon

Would you do it? Would you *dare* to compete in a Mentathlon? A *brain* competition? You might think you would, but the odds of actually doing it are slim. Do you know why? It is because you won't find any to compete in! Think about it. How long has it been since you entered your last brain competition?

What was the date of the last brain competition that was held *anywhere* in your town?

When was the last time you watched one on television?

Judging by that slightly confused look on your face, I'd say there is a good chance you have never even *heard* of a brain competition! So there you have it. The reason you won't be competing with your brain anytime soon is because there aren't any competitions for you to enter.

Doesn't that seem just a little odd to you? If it doesn't now, it will soon.

Let's take a look at competition in general. Wouldn't you agree that competition is basically a good thing for the marketplace? It keeps prices down, so doesn't that make it a good thing for the consumer?

On the other hand, *lack of competition*, like that which occurs as the result of too many mergers, *reduces selection* and leads to *higher prices*. That should easily prove that competition in the marketplace is good thing.

What about competition in sports? For instance, if you are a runner, what happens when you run against someone who is every bit as fast as you are?

You run faster.

Have you ever played tennis? What happens when you are playing against a better tennis player?

You play better tennis. And so on, and so on.

Competition *is good.*

Competition against *better players* is good.

So let me ask you this, "Do you consider intelligence to be a good thing?" Of course you do. Whether you are an adult, a child, or the parent of a child, you all know that intelligence is important. You would also probably agree that a high level of intelligence even gives you *bragging rights.* Face it, parents love those "honor student" bumper stickers. And some of you, secretly, like to think you *yourself* are just a little smarter than the "average bear." You *know* I'm right on this one. So given the fact that intelligence is important to you, and since the world presents gold medals for almost everything you can imagine, doesn't it make you wonder why "brain competitions" have never made it to the front pages? Oh sure, there is the occasional "Spelling Bee" for kids, but when was the last time you saw an I.Q. champion featured on the cover of a Wheaties box?

Never!

Here's a revelation from the *other side.* Just as fast runners make each other faster, smart minds competing with each other, *make smart minds smarter.*

Look at the physical condition of your greatest athletes. Imagine having human beings in that same condition, *mentally.* Imagine the intellectual horsepower of a Gold Medallist Olympic Mentathlete. That might sound unusual to you now, but by tomorrow it won't.

The human brain's ability to perform needs to be challenged. Without challenge it will stagnate. Most of you know stories of very smart high school graduates who later on in life never achieved what was expected of them. In many cases you will find they simply got caught in an environment and around other minds that no longer challenged and even *discouraged* their mental faculties and ambitions. Just like the runner with no more fast runners to run against, they mentally just slowed down. And you don't have to be a scholastic superstar for this to happen.

Lack of intellectual competition leads to lack of intellectual growth. How long has it been since you and your friends challenged each other to a "loser buys lunch" I.Q. test? Or logged on to the Mensa website and worked yourselves through the Mensa workout?

You've never even considered it, have you?

Thanks to me, it takes getting old for you to realize that your brain needs exercise. This is why you find elderly humans making deliberate efforts to learn something new each year. If you really want to do your elders a favor, do something creative, like establishing a legal system that hires older humans as professional jurors. This would provide them with regular mental exercise, and allow your court system to take advantage of their many years of experience and wisdom. It would also allow younger humans, those who are still trying to provide for their families, the opportunity to stay on the job where their families and their companies need them. But what do I know.

The human brain is capable of far more than any of you have been able to realize. It is a *mental conduit* to the eternal forces that created you. In certain ways, it is both the main frame and modem that connects you to the spiritual internet through which you can discover your divine purpose, which in the spirit of competition, is your greatest weapon.

And you thought it was just for remembering to pick up milk on the way home.

One of the ways in which I was able to keep human intellect on such a low profile was to go after the humans who truly understood its power. Making sure the most active minds didn't fit in with the mainstream was priceless. I made sure their hair was always a little oily, their clothes were out of fashion and that their eye glasses always sat just a little crooked on their face.

That's right, I turned them all into "Nerds." Yep. It was me. As a matter of fact, if you turn the calendar back to the early 1980's you will find one of my greatest examples of nerd-work ever! Actually, you might have already heard of him. His name is *Bill Gates.*

That darn Bill. I had him right where I wanted him. He had uncombed oily hair, a terrible wardrobe, and glasses that were never on straight. He was a powerful piece of human intellect all perfectly contained, right up to the point he stopped paying attention to outside influences and unleashed his mental ability. Bill turned loose all of his accumulated knowledge and started a company called Microsoft. Before you knew it he was off to the rich guy races. By the year 1997, Bill's intellect and ambition had become so powerful that he won the Mentathlon Gold Medal by managing to increase his net worth by 2.1 million dollars *per hour for an entire year!*

Multiply 2.1 million x 40 hours x 52 weeks. That's big cake.

If a nerd like Bill Gates can pull off a stunt like this, just think what *you* can do.

The Ego You Wish You Had

Humans can be so interesting. They will ridicule one person for having a strong ego, and then turn right around and praise someone else for having the courage to battle back from failure!

Ignorance must be bliss. It is the *ego* that *produces* the power to battle back. That is why I went after it the way I did. Come on, you know I did. Later on today if someone accuses you of having an "ego" you will squirm in your chair hoping it goes away before anyone else finds out! This was a simple deception to put together. All I did was make people think that having an ego was the same as being arrogant. The next thing you knew nobody wanted one anymore. Bada-bing bada-boom, job done.

Too easy.

If you can't bounce back from adversity and failure, you will never succeed.

Since arriving into the spirit world I've had access to incredible information on mental attributes like, positive thinking, confidence, the ego, and how they play significant roles in the overall scheme of super-achievement.

You know what they say, "Knowledge is power."

When I lived on earth I never understood how closely the ego and confidence work together, and how essential to super-achievement they both are.

Look at it this way. Consider the basic structure of an iceberg. While it is actually just *one* piece of ice, icebergs are usually referred to as though they have *two* separate pieces. The smaller portion (the tip) which is above the water, and the *larger portion* that is under the water and cannot be seen. Think of your *ego* as being the smaller portion of the iceberg. It is area that is *above the water*, which in this example, we'll refer to as the part of you that is *conscious*.

Confidence, which you will learn more about later, lives in the larger portion of the iceberg. It is the portion that is under the water. It is the area that is subsurface, or *subconscious*. But let's stay with the ego for now.

Although you've been trained to think otherwise, the ego has nothing to with being arrogant. The ego is a conscious (above the water) mental instrument intended to help you cope with the day to day realities of life. The ego is at the center of your hearing, seeing, thinking and reacting. A strong and powerful ego plays a significant role in determining how you will cope with the vast array of situations, adversities and failures that you will encounter during your lifetime.

Champion athletes can provide great examples of strong egos at work. Everyone has seen a tennis player get thrashed in their first set or two, only to see them come back to win the match in straight sets. Athletic comebacks don't happen to people with weak egos.

You don't have to be an athlete to have a strong healthy ego. One of the strongest and toughest egos to ever walk on earth belonged to a music composer from Germany named Ludwig van Beethoven.

Ludwig composed and performed some of the most brilliant music ever, and did so even though his life was more difficult than one might imagine.

Ludwig's father was an alcoholic, which made his childhood and adolescence more difficult than most. His mother died when he was eighteen years old, causing him to take the responsibility of his two younger brothers.

A short time later, just as Ludwig was becoming successful, the unthinkable occurred. Ludwig began losing his hearing.

Can you imagine composing music without the ability to hear sound? For most musicians this would be the end of their careers. But not for Ludwig. His ego was strong enough to challenge, and to conquer, any adversity.

Ludwig found that by laying his head directly on the piano he was able to detect sounds through direct vibrations. It was in this way that Ludwig van Beethoven began composing his most artistic masterpieces. And in the single greatest comeback of all time, he brought symphony to its ultimate development by composing Beethoven's Ninth, the standard by which all other composers would forever measure their work.

Just to be clear on something, I didn't cause a single problem for Beethoven. I couldn't have stopped him even if I tried because he was too mentally powerful. Besides, if he'd given up on his music, it wouldn't be around today for the rest of us to enjoy.

Beethoven had a gift, and left behind his music. You also have a gift. What will you leave behind?

A Very Scary Fish

You don't have to achieve fame or immortality to have an ego that will keep you calm in the eye of a storm.

Take a guy named Chip for example. What caught my attention about Chip was, even though he had faced a volume of intense adversity in his life, he was not only still standing, but now he was off learning to fly airplanes as though nothing bad had happened at all! People like Chip end up motivating other humans to pursue and achieve their goals, so I thought I better make a run at him.

I remember the day he made his first solo flight in an old Piper Tomahawk. The Tomahawk is an unusual looking single engine aircraft that is affectionately referred to as a "Flying Thunderchicken." Chip didn't care what the airplane looked like. He was learning to fly because he enjoyed aviation, and because he believed it was his calling… *that it was a part of his purpose for being created in the first place.*

Ironically, it would be his passion for flying that would eventually expose him to vulnerability.

Chip's first solo came on a cold winter morning with a temperature of only five degrees. He wasn't sure if his knees were shaking from his nerves, the cold temperature or from the twelve-knot crosswind that was blowing snow diagonally across the runway.

After composing himself, he keyed the microphone and radioed the control tower.

"Flying Cloud Tower, Tomahawk Zero Eight Niner Sierra, runway niner right, ready for takeoff."

The tower radioed back, "Tomahawk Zero Eight Niner Sierra, fly right traffic, runway niner right cleared for takeoff."

Chip taxied the small single engine craft onto the runway and throttled in full power. The takeoff roll and climb into the airport traffic pattern was no problem. In fact, everything had gone like clockwork until he had flown back down over the runway and the airplane was flaring to land. Flaring the airplane basically means flying nose-high just prior to touchdown. This ensures that the main landing gear touches down first as opposed to the nose gear first. Which, if the nose gear were to hit hard enough, it would break off and cause the airplane to fall into its propeller. This causes a bunch of horrible noises, gets real expensive, and is a terrific way to end a flying career before it ever gets started.

If things were going to work out as I had planned, Chip's flying career was about to come to a skidding halt.

As Chip brought the airplane down over the runway, the blowing snow and crosswinds were almost too much for a new flyer to handle. The airplane touched down hard and with too much airspeed, which caused it to hop back into the air. Feeling like it still had some flight left in it, Chip tried setting the airplane up for another flare. A nice idea but with one major problem. Chip should have added some power to ensure the plane would, absolutely, still be going fast enough to fly and control.

Well, with everything happening so fast, Chip didn't add power and the airplane didn't fly. Any useable airspeed had been scrubbed off during its hop. As Chip tried to regain control of the airplane, his efforts were of no use. The airplane's nose began falling towards the runway. The elevator of the aircraft, which is used to raise its nose, had absolutely no effect on the airplane at such a slow airspeed.

The airplane hit hard on its nose wheel. Then the main wheels hit, causing the airplane to skip nose high back into the air. And then suddenly, the entire process began to repeat itself! The nose began falling again. Chip pulled back on the elevator, but again, nothing. The nose wheel hit hard followed by the main wheels, and then the airplane skipped right back into the air again!

Chip was caught in a rare aviation event known as a "Porpoise." So named because it causes the airplane to go down the runway looking much the same as a porpoise leaping across the ocean. This may paint images in your mind of something artistic and graceful, but to porpoise an airplane is nothing of the kind!

With each hop the plane was actually skipping higher and diving more *steeply* toward the runway. And if things weren't bad enough, with every hop the airplane was being blown closer to the snowbank at the edge of the runway! (You think you've had bad days.)

I had Chip right where I wanted him. He was in an airplane that was completely uncontrollable and headed straight for a snowbank. Hey, I know what you're thinking, but this little aviation fender bender wasn't going to hurt him, physically. But it would scare him enough, or discourage him enough, to make him give up his hopes for a flying career and subsequently, give up an extremely valuable gift. Or so I thought. I still can't believe it, but in what had to be *microsecond*, Chip's mind remembered and actually processed information he had read *one time* about being caught in a porpoise. He recalled reading (in this microsecond) that when a porpoise occurs, the airplane is caught in its own kinetic energy, and will continue to hop higher and fall more steeply until it either crashes nose first, or the pilot somehow gets the airplane flying again.

That's it. You either make it fly, or crash!

In the moment these thoughts had rifled through Chip's mind, the plane had taken its last hop from the runway and was about to crash nose first into the snowbank along the edge of the runway!

"FLY!" Chip yelled out to himself.

Like the strike of a cat's paw Chip's hand shot for the throttle jamming on full power. The airplane was flying so slow it was literally *hanging* in the air. It was so low to the ground that its wheels were actually straddling the snowbank as it flew, slowly, along the edge of the runway! Chip kept the airplane low to the ground until there was enough airspeed to climb safely back up to pattern altitude.

(Perhaps a medal winning performance in a Mentathlon, don't you think?)

Once again, a human's knowledge and ability to think had really paid off. But Chip's performance was only half finished. Consider the position he was in. He was a student pilot flying through the air while so frightened he couldn't stop shaking, and at the same time, he knew he would have to fly right back down and face the same situation again! Chip wanted nothing more than to pull it over, put it in park and get out! A nice idea with an automobile, but for obvious reasons, not so in an airplane.

This presented another perfect opportunity to break him. He was alone and scared, and had absolutely nobody there to help him. I did everything I could to fill his mind with self-doubt, but the strength of Chip's ego was too much. **No matter what I threw at him, the focus of his concentration was beyond distraction.** Chip knew the airplane had to be landed and was forcing himself to shake off any fear or doubt. He mentally reviewed the proper techniques for crosswind landings. "Over the threshold, smooth power reductions, left aileron, right rudder, patient in the flare, and if you don't like it hit the power, go around and try it again."

Coming down on final approach, his teeth were gritted together as though he was about to engage in a fistfight. He would not let the fear from his near crash overcome the concentration he was giving to this second landing.

The landing was a success. In fact it turned out to be one of his best ever. From that day forward, crosswind landings became the focus of intensive study for Chip, eventually making him one of the best crosswind pilots in the business.

That's right, in the "business." Chip went on to become a professional pilot. I might have left Beethoven alone, but I took Chip to the mats, and couldn't break him. His ego is too strong. So strong in fact, that on three separate occasions he has been forced to deal with catastrophic engine failures while in flight. In all three cases Chip was able to bring his crippled airplanes, and everyone on board, home safely. Today he flies high performance jets at 45,000 feet in the air traveling over 500 miles per hour. I guess you could say Chip is *succeeding at the speed of sound*.

With everything that has happened in his life, when Chip isn't flying he spends his time presenting motivational lectures. He enjoys encouraging people to reach for the impossible, to conquer adversity and achieve their goals. He's pretty good at it too, which is all the more reason that I'm glad I am retiring soon. As a matter of fact, do you remember that speaker guy I mentioned who was talking about walking through walls?

Yep. It's Chip.

An Ego Named "Spalding"

Thanks to me, there are people just like you spending millions each year on therapy. I am not talking about physical therapy to heal a bad back. I'm talking about *mental* therapy.

Here's a tip. Strong egos require less therapy. If you are wondering why some of you have trouble bouncing back from adversity, perhaps you have never heard about the "Ego of the Bouncing Ball."

Picture two balls sitting on a shelf. For our purposes, let's say the balls are the size of basketballs. Now, if you can imagine it, instead of the balls being filled with air pressure, they are filled with *ego* pressure. The balls represent people, and the shelf they are sitting on represents the general plane of life that you live on most of the time. The floor beneath the shelf represents the place where you fall to during times of crisis, problems, or defeat.

The first ball, while it might look fine on the outside, has a weak ego. We'll say that it has "low" ego pressure. Having defined the ego as something that will help you cope, or *bounce back*, from daily problems and difficulties, you could say that this low ego pressure ball does not possess much of an ability to bounce back from setbacks. What do you suppose happens when this low ego (pressure) ball falls from the shelf and hits the floor? It falls to the floor easily enough, but then with a disheartening "thud" it stays there. It doesn't have enough of what it takes to bounce itself, or to bring itself, back up to where it was before the fall. As the ball spends time on the floor, just as when a human is depressed, a fortune in gifts and assets lay idle and unused.

Now let's look at the other ball on the shelf. This ball has "high" ego pressure. Like the other ball, it also encounters problems and setbacks. However this ball reacts differently. When the high-pressure ball falls from the shelf, it too hits the floor, but only for a moment. With its higher pressure (stronger ego) the second ball has the ability to face up to its setbacks and bounce itself back up to the shelf! In fact, the harder it slams to the floor, the higher it bounces!

People with strong egos are able to conquer adversity and make good use of what they have been given. If you are one of these people you should consider yourself fortunate, except for one thing...

Do you hear that *hissing* sound?

The Big Half of the Iceberg

Out of sight out of mind. Just as it is with the larger and more powerful half of an iceberg, so it is with the human subconscious… the place where confidence lives. But since you can't see it, feel it or touch it, like so many other things, humans tend to forget it is there.

The subconscious is powerful beyond explanation. You've all heard of situations like those when a woman lifts an automobile off of her trapped husband. Medical doctors attribute this type of super-human act to the stimulation of the adrenal glands. This is true, except it is the *subconscious* that is *causing* the stimulation of the adrenal glands. The subconscious is communicating, or, *taking command* of the body, and when this happens anything is possible. That's why I've worked so hard to pull the plug on this kind of communication.

When I don't, humans taste a little too much success.

Humans get a little reluctant with the entire conscious/subconscious thing, so let me put this in some fairly common, every day terms.

Did you ever learn to type? Do you remember those first few weeks of practicing? When you consider the process, it is a very conscious activity that sounds something like this, "Left index finger is the 'F', right ring finger is the, um, 'I', yea that's it the 'I'," and so on, as you work your way up to 12-words per minute. This is a great example of *conscious* activity. Every letter, every movement of your finger, carefully, consciously, thought through.

Compare that process to someone who has put in thousands of hours at a keyboard. Have you ever watched someone who is cruising at 60 to 80-words per minute? These people are not consciously thinking to themselves, "Right ring finger for the 'l'."

Their subconscious has them typing in *pictures*. In other words, when they look at the document they are typing, their eyes send a picture of the words they are looking at and the subconscious moves the correct finger for them. They are not thinking consciously. They are in a sense, *unconscious*. After thousands of hours of typing, their subconscious is able to take complete control.

Have you done something, anything, and after finishing it you thought to yourself, "Everything just clicked." A time when you were, "In the zone." Those were subconscious experiences.

A good example of this can be made with the true story about a karate student named, Rod.

Rod was a 24-year old athlete who became very enthusiastic about the martial arts. He worked extremely hard at it, putting in very long hours.

When Rod entered his first tournament his hard work paid off. He finished in first place in the beginner division, and took home a gold medal. And so it would continue into the future. Extremely hard work followed by a gold medal for the effort.

Rod quickly worked his way to the level of black belt, and shortly thereafter was competing in a tournament to determine the National Champion.

Rod never worked harder preparing for a tournament. While warming up before the competition was to begin, a fellow competitor asked Rod how he was going to perform that day. Rod responded, with eyes of steel framed within an expressionless face, "This is my tournament."

It didn't take long before some of the other competitors were making comments about how arrogant he must be to make a comment like that.

Point number one, did they expect him to say something like, "I have worked harder than anyone else who is here to today. I hope I lose"?

Point number two, unlike confidence, arrogance is false pride and is not recognized by the subconscious. Confidence *lives* there. When a competitor makes a statement out of arrogance all he or she is doing is talking, which for the most part is a conscious activity. As far as the subconscious is concerned, they are false statements and the competitor will lose. How do you know for sure? Just check the outcomes. Rod entered two events and won the gold medal in both. In just three years he had gone from beginner to National Champion, taking a first place finish in every tournament he had ever entered.

Let me try to make all these comments about "consciousness" a little more clear.

When competing in a karate tournament (or doing something like typing 80-words per minute) there is no time for conscious decision making. In such a lightening fast competition, whatever needs to happen has to happen automatically, or the competitor will lose. These kinds of incredibly high-speed responses are called *trained reactions* and only occur through the subconscious. The only way your subconscious is able to generate and execute the correct reaction is if it has been given the proper training and knowledge to do so!

By the time Rod had entered the national championships he had trained for thousands of hours. He had every right to feel confident. He wasn't concerned about being able to talk a good fight. He wasn't too concerned about thinking at all! Rod was able to discover something that I was able to keep from the other competitors. He had learned that if he tried to consciously think and decide every move he was going to make, he would be too slow. Instead, he knew that if he did a good job of training the right movements into his subconscious, all he would have to do is relax, let his mind remain clear, and let his subconscious react the way it was trained to. Any conscious interfering on his part would only slow him down.

Do you want to know the difference in speed between a conscious movement and a reaction? While sitting there, try to move your head to the right as fast as you can. Note the speed of your movement. Now, think back to a time when someone had thrown a football at your head that you didn't know was coming. At the last second you heard someone yell, "Look out!" You turned your head to see what they are alerting you to, only to discover a football traveling at light speed and only 3-inches from you nose! It *misses* because your subconscious *reacted* by moving your head.

Which head movement was faster?

Think about the last time you took out a pen and wrote your name. Do you know what was happening when you did? You pictured your signature, your hand went whoosh, and there it was! You pictured it and your subconscious caused your body to make it happen! It was able to do this because you've signed your name so many times that it has become, "automatic." If someone where to ask you, "Will you be able to write your name today?" and you responded by saying, "Yes I will," would that be arrogant on your part? Of course not, because writing your name has become a trained subconscious response. If you don't believe that, just think back to how slow and difficult it was when you were first learning to print!

See what I mean?

Just as you can be confident in the fact that you know how to write your name, with enough training you can become confident in your ability to do anything else, which is why I keep telling you things like, "That's good enough." It limits your production and negatively impacts the training of the subconscious.

Remember the woman who lifted the automobile off of her husband? How many times in her life do you suppose she had knelt down to lift something? Probably thousands of times, right? In other words, she *knew* how to lift things. **When the car fell off the jack onto her husband, what do you think would have happened if she would have taken the time to consciously think to herself, "I can't lift a car, it's too heavy"?** It would have been a tragedy. Instead, her subconscious made her react, as quickly as ducking a football, before she had time for any negative conscious thinking. The larger portion of the iceberg instantly took over, and her husband was saved.

Every human has the potential for this kind of super-human performance. It is inside of you at this moment. If you don't believe me, go write your name and few times. I'll be waiting for you when you finish.

Robert Bakke

Where Money Comes From

If parents honestly understood the young age at which money becomes important to their children, they would be less likely to judge their children's goals on their adult scale, and instead, react to them with excitement and support. The reason adults react the way they do to the financial curiosities of children, is because I've got most of them convinced that having enough money to retire is somehow related to old age. But the fact is, *retirement is not a matter of age, it is a matter of income.* Growing old has nothing to do with it. If little humans were encouraged to begin learning about making the big chips while they were still children, it would in-turn begin producing an abundance of teenaged millionaires, virtually super-charging the earth's economy. But if you're appalled at the idea of teaching financial strategies to children, here's something you may want to think about trying.

Find a large classroom filled with grade school children. Ask the entire class how many of them want to grow up to become *teachers*. Do you know what will happen? Two or three kids will raise their hands. Ask the class how many want to become *construction workers*. Two or three will raise their hands. Ask the class how many of them want to become *pilots*. Two or three kids will raise their hands. Now, ask the class how many of them want to grow up and make *tons of money*. The entire class will explode with activity!

Go ahead and try it. You will quickly discover that when it comes to having enough money, you are all more similar than you realize. But then again, since you're all less than one-second apart perhaps that makes sense.

Doesn't it seem odd that most adults will admit that planning for retirement should start early, yet they overlook teaching financial planning matters to children (as do most schools), and compound the problem by putting off the start of their own retirement savings until they are in their forties! It is easy to talk the talk, but thanks to me it is often more difficult to walk the walk.

Another element to explore in the process of money making can be learned from the story of the impatient karate student.

There was once a karate student who attended a few karate classes, read a few karate books, and then decided to train with the great master. In order to do this he traveled to the country of Japan. After arriving in the new country, he asked the great master if the master would teach him. The great master agreed, and asked the student to change into his karate uniform and then meet him in the training area. The student agreed and a few minutes later they were ready to begin.

The great master began the lesson by saying, "First you must learn to punch." Then, just as the master began to demonstrate a punch, the student abruptly cut off the master's sentence saying, "Yea, I know." He then demonstrated a poorly executed punch of his own.

The master stepped back, regrouped his thoughts and said politely, "Perhaps I will teach you to kick." Again, just as the master began to demonstrate a kick, the student again cut him off saying, "Yea, I know," and proceeded to demonstrate his own terrible kicking technique.

The master quietly turned and left the training area, returning a moment later with two cups of water. After handing the student one of the cups, the master held his cup over the cup the student was now holding, and began pouring the water from his cup into the already full cup of the student's. The cold water began flowing over the top of the student's cup and splashing down onto his bare feet, to which student jumped back yelling, "Stop it!"

The master then reached over and took the student's cup away from him, dumped out the water, and handed the empty cup back to the student. The master then, without saying word, reached over and began pouring the remainder of his water into the empty cup the student was now holding. **The water flowed easily into the empty cup.**

The student looked at the master and with a hint of disgust said, "I don't get it. What's your point?" The master replied, **"Before you can learn what I have to teach you, you must first empty your cup."**

What does this have to do with making money? Look at it this way. Imagine your brain as a giant container with a big open lid on top. Each day as you learn new things, that knowledge goes into your container. The more knowledge you put into your container, the more valuable your container, your *mind*, becomes to others. In many ways, you can look at your mind as a mental bank account. The more you put into it, the more valuable it becomes. That's why I do what I can to stop you from listening and learning, because when you do, the lid closes and stops valuable information from getting inside. In other words, if you want a single-word answer to the secret of making money, I'll give it to you. That single word is *knowledge*.

Knowledge **is where money comes from.**

Boring, right? Of course it is, and that's why the coolest kids in school grow up to be poor adults with terrible jobs. Why? It's because they have no knowledge to sell. They fail to develop a specialized area of specific, abundant, *sellable* knowledge. An area of "expertise." They could have done it in banking, accounting, business, law, medicine, sales or any number of other areas, but they didn't.

Knowledge is where money comes from, because your knowledge is what people *pay you for*. People pay you for things *you* know, or know how to do, that *they* don't.

I know that sounds *real* complicated.

Let's talk more about cool kids. Do you know what makes a lot of cool kids, cool? It's because they think they know more than other people, particularly adults. More specifically, they think they know more than *teachers* do. So do you know what happens next? I make them stop listening. They close their ears. They close the lid on their container and stop learning.

The fact that anyone believes they know everything is a testimony to the quality of my work. Your mind is a container so large that you won't use more than a tiny fraction of its space while you are here on earth. (Keep in mind that you have an eternity of learning ahead of you, so don't worry about running out of room any time soon.) That makes the thought of knowing everything, particularly at the age of let's say, fifteen, overwhelmingly ignorant.

Regardless of what your age is, the moment you catch yourself impatiently uttering those special words, "Yea, I *know*," to someone, remember that you are essentially *burning* future revenues. It's like throwing a match to dollars that could have ended up in your wallet.

Let's go back to the earlier example of the big house on the lake with an expensive powerboat and a Dodge Viper in the garage. Next time you begin thinking you know everything, start asking yourself what it is that you know that is *so* valuable, that someone will pay you enough money to support your lifestyle on the lake?

Well, what is it? Your lifestyle on the lake is going to cost at least a few hundred thousand a year, so what is it that you know that is worth that kind of money to someone?

If you are a 15-year old *know it all*, what is it that you know that is going to put a Dodge Viper in the garage? If you are a 50-year old know it all, ask yourself the same question.

In 1975 there was a really cool kid that graduated from high school. He had been cool ever since the 7th grade. He knew it all. Today that cool kid is 43-years old and is a *full time* Domino's Pizza delivery driver. A true story.

Obviously there is nothing wrong with delivering pizzas to work your way through school, or to earn a few extra bucks to help pay for something like a new snowmobile. But this guy's full-time delivery status is as far as he has been able to make it. Do you know why? Because he stopped listening as a teenager and at that age there isn't much in your container to sell.

Do you know what he should have done? Back when he was in school, he should have looked at his report card as a paycheck. After all, they look about the same. They are both made of paper, and have printing on them. The only difference between them is that a report card has *letters* (A, B, C), and paychecks have *numbers*. But whether they have letters or numbers, they are reflective of the same thing. They are indicators of the *amount* and *value* of the sellable knowledge you have in your mental piggy bank.

In most cases, *low grades* on a report card later become *low numbers* on a paycheck. Conversely, *high grades* usually become *high numbers* on a paycheck. So if you are a young person still in school, next time you are sitting in class, spin around in your chair and check out the back row. You know the one. The row where the cool kids sit with their heads down on their desks. *These* are my people! Yep, the future 40-year old pizza delivery drivers of America!

Pyramid Power-less

Perhaps it has been in the back of your mind for a while now. Opening your own business, setting your own hours, finally getting paid what you are worth, achieving wealth and financial independence. You want it so bad you can taste it, and that's exciting.

When it is time to begin making your moves toward independent riches there is something that, *mysteriously*, very few people take time to consider. It is called, "Getting Rich Slowly and Carefully," which we will discuss in detail in the next chapter. It is a far cry from the *Get Rich Quick* pyramid schemes that are out there, and it might mean dumping the monster mortgage payment and the leased BMW (unless it's an M3, you never dump an M3), but the odds of success are nearly 100%. Nonetheless, building wealth this way takes a long time to do and most humans don't like that, so they pay little attention to the slow *guaranteed* approach, and focus on quicker methods.

Or do they?

If someone called tonight and asked you to attend a meeting on home businesses or one of those *multi-level* pyramid programs, would you go? Nope! And with good cause, because they usually don't work. But *should* they work? That is the big question.

Examine the pyramid concept and compare it the management structure of the company you work for right now. In fact, compare it to the management structure of any company you have worked for. You will find a pyramid that has a president at the top, a few vice presidents under him or her, with a larger number of regional directors under them, and so on, spreading out at the bottom, ultimately forming the shape of a pyramid.

The only difference between the pyramid structure of the company you work for and the pyramid structure of a multi-level marketing (MLM) company is that your company's profits don't flow proportionately down through the ranks, but in the MLM pyramid they are supposed to. Sound good? It should.

Do you remember the "multiply your efforts through other people" principle of the Lawnmower Millions? There are few better places to put that principle to work than in an MLM company, because MLM is all about generating revenue through the efforts of others.

You may think that getting involved in multi-level marketing is crazy, but what is *more* crazy? Investing a couple hundred dollars to give a home business a try, or risking your life savings at the age of *fifty* in a high overhead, labor intensive retail or manufacturing business?

When you look at the dangers and pitfalls of starting your own business, multi-level marketing should be the ticket to the American dream! But thanks to me, it's not. The concept had so much potential that I just had to go after it.

My efforts to ruin multi-level marketing have enjoyed remarkable success. Face it, if your telephone rings tonight with an invitation to attend an MLM meeting, you won't go. I rest my case.

So how did I do it? It was simple, as soon as I saw the potential of these programs I made everyone involved start telling people the most absurd things. Things like how an MLM company would help them, "Get rich quick." Which as you have obviously figured out, is ridiculous. I also made them tell people that it's, "Easy money." This is just as ridiculous, and creates the tendency to attract people who aren't willing to put in long hours. If you want to make the big bucks you better be prepared to work your butt off.

Speaking of hard work, one of the Ivy League universities did a study to determine if self-made millionaires are actually *smarter* than other humans.

The study revealed that a typical self-made millionaire is not necessarily separated by their intelligence, but by an extreme difference in their work ethic! The study determined that the most significant attribute separating self-made millionaires from other humans is that they are willing to study longer and *work harder* than other humans.

What a concept.

Sorry to break it to you, but there is no such thing as quick, *easy* money. Big money is the result of big effort.

My final dagger to the MLM concept came by making multi-level marketers invite people to meetings where everyone *pretends* they are making big bucks even though they aren't, and then, like nails on a chalkboard, they yell and cheer and wave their arms around, celebrating the money they haven't made! Real professional.

If they put that much energy into actually selling products, they might actually be as rich as they like to tell people they are.

By the time I was done I had successfully put the "scam" in pyramid, and had shut down the potential of what was once a truly clever idea.

Robert Bakke

More Money

Than You Can Spend

You can't fault someone for wanting to step out of the mainstream and blaze a trail into their own business. Consider your dream lifestyle. If the job you are working today isn't going to provide the resources necessary to attain it, then you have to do something else. You may have to change jobs. Perhaps get more education, or maybe even start your own business. Sure it's risky, but it might be your only way to generate enough income to achieve that dream lifestyle of yours. The bottom line is, if you want a better lifestyle than your current job can provide for, then you have to do *something*, or give up your dream.

Starting your own business will also provide access to tax deductions that you wouldn't otherwise be entitled to.

Speaking of taxes, here is a little eye opener on why tax deductions are so important. What do you think is the single largest expense for most businesses?

It is the payroll.

How do you suppose the government comes up with the money to make *their* payroll?

It comes right out of your pocket! In fact, by the time you receive your paycheck the money is already gone! They don't *ask* you for the money.

92

They don't *invoice* you for the money. They just take the money! In the ghetto that's referred to as a *"Jack!"*

Big government means big taxes. Big taxes keep you financially suppressed, and that keeps a lot of people from venturing out and trying new things. If you want to know how successful I have been at growing big government, let me ask you this. How large do you suppose the government's payroll really is? Come on, take a guess. How many people do you think your hard hours of labor are really supporting? Here is a small sample.

Let's suppose you live in the state of Minnesota. With all of the businesses that are located there, check out the two largest.

#1. The United States Government

#2. The State of Minnesota

YIKES! Don't you find it a little concerning that a state's two largest employers are both government organizations whose massive payrolls are paid out of your hard-earned dollars? That's just *one* state! Keep in mind that the payroll expense, while it might be the single largest expense, is only one of thousands of other government expenses that are all coming out of your paycheck! With overhead like that, don't expect your taxes to come down too far on their own. All the more reason why having a business of your own and creating tax deductions to shelter your income (which means *you* keep more of *your* money) makes all the more sense.

So in the quest for wealth and financial independence, you have multi-level marketing, which I have successfully harpooned. You could also try a mainstream business like retail or manufacturing, but this will require a greater up front investment and present much greater financial risks. However, if it is something you really want to do, and you don't try, it will never happen.

Finally, you can consider the *least* popular way to achieve wealth and independence. It is the financial plan called, "Getting Rich Slowly and Carefully."

What's interesting about Getting Rich Slowly and Carefully is that it combines many of the areas previously discussed, and provides almost guaranteed success.

Getting rich slowly begins with the understanding that, as was discussed earlier, you must develop something that is of value to someone else. That means amassing an area of knowledge and expertise that someone will pay you handsomely to obtain. You then find this someone and *immediately* go to work for them! "Immediately" because *time* is of the essence.

I realize that this might sound like going out and getting a job. However, instead of looking at it as a job, you need to look at it as going into business for yourself, but doing it in a way that makes *someone else* pay all of your expenses. Think about it. If you were going to market yourself by opening your own office, just think of the overhead you would incur! By having someone *hire* you for your expertise, instead of you paying for everything on your own, your employer pays all of your expenses. They pay the rent for the building you are working in, and provide the carpeted floors that you walk on. When it's hot outside, *they* pay for the air conditioning. When it's cold outside, they pay for the heat! They also provide you with a desk, a computer, a telephone, fax, internet access, copier and other office supplies. These are all things that you would have to pay for by yourself if you were on your own. Plus, most of these companies provide medical insurance (a huge benefit) and above all, a 401k retirement plan.

Be sure any company you work for offers a 401k retirement plan, because this is your ticket to long term financial stardom. Yes, I realize the market has fallen since the 90's, but keep in mind that money is made by investing when the markets are down! *Now is that time.* So stay with me here, because you're about to become your own investment banker, and will be working with numbers you haven't yet begun to imagine.

Once you have begun generating an income, you need to acquire two *career* financial planners (as opposed to piano teachers turned financial planners). Select them from different companies, and do it as soon as you can. Have one financial planner help you with your pre-taxed 401k dollars, and the other with the after-taxed dollars you receive in your paycheck. Got it? One for your 401K, and one for your paycheck dollars.

Next, have each of the two planners help you select *three,* possibly *four,* different mutual funds for you to invest your dollars into. Two planners with three or four funds each, makes a total of *six* to *eight* mutual funds. This creates financial diversity, and offers good protection from wild fluctuations in the market.

Presto! You just created your own financial pyramid! (I told you they were a good idea). There you are on top of the pyramid, just like a company president. Under you there are two financial planners. Under each of them there is a grouping of mutual funds. Below each mutual fund are hundreds or perhaps thousands of individual stocks that make up each of the funds. A perfect pyramid. A revenue generating machine. Just as it was with the Lawnmower Millions, so it is here. Except in this case you're not multiplying your efforts through having other people mow lawns. Instead, you're multiplying your efforts through mutual funds, because every minute that you are at work, every tiny stock of every single mutual fund is out there compounding interest for you. Literally *generating* money for you. Don't sell this process short. In the next few minutes you will see small numbers grow into enough millions to keep you awake for a very long time.

Now, I realize that many of you are all caught up playing, "Keeping broke with the Jones'." This could mean that you don't have too much extra money to invest, but look at it this way. I'm the one who pushed you into building those giant houses you think you have to live in, and pressured you into leasing vehicles you couldn't otherwise afford to be driving. Since I am the one who pushed society into this situation, perhaps I am the one who should get society out of this situation.

What?

You didn't like me taking a shot at your house? Well then, *run the numbers*. Let's suppose the social pressure of your friend's debt has caused your own common sense to buckle, and now there you sit with your own $200,000.00 mortgage. (Correct me if I'm wrong, but we were talking about financial *independence*, right?)

Do you realize (excluding whatever your down payment was) that your $200,000.00 mortgage is probably going to cost around $500,000.00 (or more) to payback over thirty years? That's prior to property taxes of let's say, oh, another $150,000.00 easy. That puts you up to about $650,000.00 before insurance, maintenance and utilities. So let's tack on at least another $150,000.00.

Let's see, that means your $200,000.00 mortgage will cost you around $800,000.00 by the time you have paid it off. So, over the length of your mortgage if the value of your home *doubles* to somewhere around $400,000.00, that means you only finish $400,000.00 in the hole!

Great investing!

Maybe you'll be lucky and the value of your house will *triple!* That will mean you only finish $200,000.00 in the hole!

Another great investment! When I was on earth I *dreamed* of spending my entire life paying for something that would leave me hundreds of thousands of dollars upside down...

On the flip side to the house thing, I realize that keeping a roof over your head should cost you *something,* and that many of you are willing to pay a little extra for a particular lifestyle. But if a person stops playing "Keeping Broke with the Jones'" and considers living in a smaller house that is less expensive, the following will *blow you away.*

Consider what happens financially when you choose a smaller, less expensive house and *invest the difference* between the cost of the two houses.

If you reduce your $800,000.00 house investment by 30%, you free up $240,000.00 to invest over the length of your thirty-year mortgage. That breaks down to $8000.00 per year, or $667.00 per month. If that sounds like a lot of money to free up for investing, just remember this. If you have a $200,000.00 mortgage, you're already paying that out every month!

If you don't think you can trim your housing by the full 30%, then you might have to dump the leased $35,000.00 gas guzzling Sport Utility Vehicle and drive something in the $24,000 range in order to hit $667.00 per month.

Look at it this way. If you live in a two-income household that means you have four paychecks coming in each month. $667.00 divided by four checks is only $166.75 per check. This is not a lot to ask in exchange for millions, do you think?

Trust what I'm saying here and begin reducing your cost of living immediately. **If you do this, and have the discipline to invest the money you'll be saving, at the end of your mortgage you will have the millions to pay cash for your new dream home, play golf every day and still** leave a *fortune* to your kids, as opposed to those who don't take my advice and end up *living* with their kids.

Carrying debt to appear successful will not make you rich. It will make you old and poor. You don't have to let that happen.

Before you get too depressed, let's get back to your banking business so you can begin financially outperforming those in-debt friends of yours.

Like I said earlier, use financial planner #1 to help you invest your 401k dollars, and immediately begin investing at least 10% of your income into these funds. That's right, ten percent! Some of you will get upset with that, but you have to remember that this 10% is not money you are losing! It's money you are *investing* to make you wealthy. *The other aspect of the 401k plan that you must pay attention to is that the dollars you invest into your 401k are not taxed! This creates your first tax shelter.*

Your second tax shelter is created by the fact that the interest your 401k dollars are generating isn't taxed either! All taxes are deferred until later on when you begin taking the money out. Until then, as your pile of 401k dollars continues to multiply upon itself, it keeps generating more and more dollars, year after year, without the government coming along and scooping money out every twelve months. With a regular savings account the government taxes your interest every year, constantly slowing your money's growth.

Finally, let's put some real numbers to this. Let's say you are 25-years old, married, and have a two-income household. If each of you invests just a meager $3000.00 per year into your 401K, here is what happens. Based on the S&P's historical interest average, at the end of thirty years you will each have a 401k minimum of $662,740.00 for a combined total of $1,325,480.00. I say "minimum" because most employers have a "matching program" with their 401k plans, which means that for every dollar *you* invest (up to a certain percentage), *they match the investment dollar for dollar, and put those dollars into your account!* That's free money! The $1,325,480.00 I showed you isn't reflective of those dollars, which means the actual amount could be higher!

So there you are. As a married couple at the ages of twenty-five, you just made yourself millionaires at the age of fifty-five. But watch this.

Let's talk about those $667.00 cost of living dollars that we trimmed out of the budget. Based on the same S&P historical interest average, at the end of your thirty-year mortgage those dollars will amount to $978,767.00! Add that to your $1,325,480.00 and at the age of fifty-five you and your spouse can retire with $2,304,247.00 *and* with your first house paid off!

But that's nothing...

Suppose you kept this going for another ten years? And keep in mind that your house is now paid off. That means the money you have been paying into your mortgage is now money you can blow! So, go buy a new Mercedes with those dollars and keep working to sixty-five, because in ten more years the interest tables cause your money to *explode.*

In ten additional years, your 401k plans are each worth $1,937,481.00 making your combined total a comfortable $3,874,962.00.

But that's *still* nothing...

While you're riding around in your new Mercedes and continuing to invest that other $670.00 per month, at the end of ten more years that $670.00 per month will amass an amazing $5,166,615.00.

Add to that to your 401k dollars in the amount of $3,874,962.00 and you have a combined total of $9,041,577.00 (minus fees and other charges).

Nine million dollars!

Like I said earlier. Follow my advice and you will have enough money to pay cash for your dream home, play golf every day and leave a fortune to your kids.

Looking back on it, I've worked very hard to keep the general public from realizing how easy it is to make huge dollars over the course of a lifetime. It seems a shame for me to undo so much hard work, but I know it is the right thing to do. So, I'll be a kind spirit and give you a couple of warnings. Here they are.

If you take even a small amount of money out of these accounts prior to achieving the timetables I laid out for you, you'll blow it! Even if you are sure you will pay the money back, the interest tables will be destroyed. Don't do it!

Secondly, after I retire I'll keep some carrot dangling going on over at the Convention Center. Like the Home Show, the Car Show, and most importantly, the Boat Show. After looking at the Ranger bass boats, the Malibu ski boats, and the Sea Ray cabin cruisers, be careful or your mutual funds will be toast! So remember, W-I-L-L-P-O-W-E-R.

The Blunder Years

Living in the spirit world gives me the chance to visit with the spirits of all kinds of historically interesting humans. One of my favorites is the achievement psychologist Dr. Abraham Maslow.

Maslow believed that when you become truly satisfied with your life you achieve a state of mind he entitled, "Self-Actualization." Self-Actualization is the fifth and final stage of a psychological progression now known as, "Maslow's Hierarchy of Needs." Maslow's theory behind the hierarchy was that the anxiety of an unmet need produces the motivation required for you to actively fulfill the unmet need. The progression of the various needs of the hierarchy are explained as follows.

THE PROGRESSION

				SELF-ACTUALIZATION
			SELF-ESTEEM	Fulfillment
		LOVE	Financial	of
	SAFETY	Affection	success	Potential
PHYSICAL	Security	Acceptance	Prestige	
Food	Comfort	Friendship	Recognition	
Water				

According to Maslow, you begin the hierarchy by filling your most basic needs first (physical and safety), and then move step by step through the progression. Upon reaching the final stage of "Self-Actualization" you begin experiencing your true potential for the very first time. Maslow also believed that this fifth and final stage could *only* be achieved after the first four stages of the progression had been satisfied.

There are a couple things to consider about the hierarchy. First of all, the hierarchy is surprisingly accurate. Abe Maslow was no dummy. Secondly, as I had mentioned a moment ago, he believed unmet needs created anxiety which, in-turn, generates the motivation to fulfill the unmet need. Also fairly accurate, until I became involved.

THE REGRESSION

Abe Maslow would have been more accurate to say that unmet needs were *supposed* to create the anxiety that causes you to fulfill your unmet needs. That was before I began causing people to stumble into the *Blunder Years.* This all got started back when I first began inviting you folks up to the lake for a little La La Land R & R. Humans started spending a little too much time at the cabin and before they knew it their dreams had completely slipped away. Others got all warm and cozy spending too much time in their *comfort zones.* That's a big problem because there isn't any anxiety or risk in a comfort zone, which means there isn't any achievement, either. Others began listening to people who said their dreams were too exceptional, and so they began settling for mediocrity. All of my success in these areas wound up really giving ol' Maslow the short end of the stick.

It's a sad thing, but all that time Maslow was working so hard to create his hierarchy, I was working just as hard to make sure he wouldn't find anyone who had actually been able to complete it. In the end, Maslow spent the balance of his life searching for self-actualized adults and couldn't find any! Well, that's not *exactly* true. He did find a few. But come on, *millions* and *millions* of you, and only a handful are experiencing your true potential?

Get ready for that "I could have had a V8" forehead slap.

While it's true (check the facts) that Maslow could only find a handful of self-actualized humans, it only turned out that way because he spent too much time researching *adult* humans.

When I told that to Maslow he looked at me funny.

That's when I told him there had been millions of self-actualized *children* everywhere around him.

Go ahead and do the V8 forehead slap. Maslow did.

Maslow had spent his time searching for self-actualized adults, rarely considering the mental framework that existed within the world's children.

Ironically, most of the adults Maslow had spent his time studying had actually self-actualized as children, but had regressed or *de-actualized* by the time he had met them.

The best way to describe a self-actualized child is to say that they are a child still living in the "wonder years." The years in which they still know and believe what most adults have forgotten. They are still aware that *anything is possible*.

Do you know what separates a self-actualized child from a de-actualized adult? The child will say, "I can be President." The adult will reply, "I will never be President." This is a classic example of what happens when you spend your time defining your *limitations* instead of your potential.

One of a child's greatest assets is their unawareness of limitations. This is a positive and constructive unawareness that protects children from learning to give up on exceptional expectations. Keep in mind that giving up on exceptional expectations is a *learned* behavior.

Perhaps you should more carefully consider the hierarchy as it might relate to children. Take a look at each of the different steps. First of all, children are dependent upon their parents for a number of items that make up the first three stages of the hierarchy. They are given *Physical* items such as food and water, *Safety* items such as security and comfort, and *Love* items such as affection and acceptance. Children also get a break on the fourth stage called "Self-Esteem." Children are not only supported financially by their parents, but they are also innocently *unaware* of things such as prestige and recognition due to personal financial success. Children don't have anxiety over financial success because it hasn't developed into a *personal need* yet. They might have a clear and emotional understanding that money is important, but they haven't figured out exactly how it is earned or where it comes from. Without money having yet become a personal *need*, there is little anxiety over having to fill it. This gives a little human with a set of loving parents an open door straight to Self-Actualization.

Unfortunately for most children, the priceless state of self-actualization doesn't last long enough. With the onset of formalized education the child's interaction with other children and other adults increases tremendously. They are constantly being evaluated both physically and scholastically to determine how they compare to other children. They are judged by how well they conform to *mainstream expectations* that may or may not be any part of what the child's natural destiny is meant to be. Peer pressure reaches new heights. The child's worth is judged in gym class based on their physical attributes. Between classes they are respected or rejected based on the label of the clothes they are wearing. But most critically, every day that they express their self-actualized vision of becoming something exceptional, their dreams are confronted with laughter. Soon, the enthusiasm of their divine destiny will begin slowly fading, and at this moment the child's de-actualization has begun.

Preventing de-actualization places a lot of responsibility on parents. If a child's self-actualization is going to be protected and retained, it has to happen at home. That presents a bit of a quandary for most parents, because while most parents want the best for their children, most parents are also adults. *Most adults have de-actualized.* They have long since given up on the fact that they could have been President, or that they could have *walked on the moon*, or become multi-millionaire entrepreneurs.

It is difficult for someone who is de-actualized to *encourage* or to even understand someone who isn't, so I've decided to be a good spirit and give you parents a few tips. First of all, hire a baby sitter for the weekend and get out of town.

Way out of town.

Once you're there, forget everything you think is important right now and make every effort to mentally return to your youth. *Rediscover* your childhood. Perhaps find the one you didn't have. Most importantly, bring your mind back to the *wonder years.*

It is essential for you *and for your children* that you remember what it was like to believe that you can do *anything.*

Challenge yourself to touch the enthusiasm that has long since slipped away. Relive the excitement of the dreams and goals you had as a child. It will not only help you to re-believe in the goals you once had the courage to imagine, but more importantly, it will help you to save the dreams your children are having today.

Perhaps it's time for another true story.

Rick was a boy about the age of four. Like other children his age, he relied on his parents for food, shelter, love and protection. He was also dependent on them at times when he wanted something from the toy store. Like most loving parents, as much as they wanted to provide for their son's every want and need, there were times when they just had to say, "No."

One of those days came on Rick's tenth birthday. Rick wanted a go-kart more than anything else in the world, but no matter how hard he *pleaded* with his parents, they would not give in. Rick continued to pressure them, until his father finally conceded that Rick could have a go-kart provided he paid for it *himself.*

Because Rick was only ten years old, his father was sure this would put an end to Rick's craving for the silly little machine that neither he nor Rick's mother wanted him to have. But rarely have two parents been so oblivious to the potential of youth. Rick was immediately hard at work cleaning garages, washing cars and raking leaves. That winter he was outside shoveling driveways and sidewalks. He was doing everything he could to earn money. The following spring, not sure if they were excited, proud or frightened, Rick's parents found themselves driving their son to the sporting goods store where he was going to buy a go-kart with his own, hard earned money.

Every time Rick climbs aboard his go-kart he feels what it is like to be self-actualized. He set a goal that he was determined to achieve, and he made it happen.

I can already read the minds of the parents out there. You're thinking that there is more to life than a silly little go-kart, and besides that they're dangerous, right? Don't tell me you're not thinking that way because I am the one who *taught* you to think that way. I am also the one who will teach you this:

You might think there is more to *your* life than a go-kart, but this is about *Rick's* life, and he is only *ten years old!* As he grows older his goals and dreams will *grow larger.* If he can hold on to the way he feels right now it will help him to attain other goals, *larger* goals, later in life.

Unfortunately, there is a very good chance that Rick's self-actualization will weaken, causing the *pride of his accomplishment* to slowly slip away. There are too many people around him who don't share the excitement of his achievement. People who don't believe something as insignificant as a go-kart or the future accomplishments it will lead to, are worthy of their support. Instead, they will continue to judge Rick's youthful dreams on their de-actualized *adult scale*, very possibly causing Rick to de-actualize. You better hope he doesn't.

You have to understand that there are a lot of Ricks out there right now. Self-actualized young people with enough dreams and determination to change the world. Do you know why they have the power to do it? **It is because the self-actualized children of today will become the entrepreneurs of tomorrow, who in-turn, become the providers of employment for the rest of the world.**

Self-actualized children learn to provide for themselves. They don't need to worry about growing up and "finding a job." These are the little humans who will grow up and *create their own jobs*, and in doing so create the jobs that the rest of you are working right now. It's the Ricks out there who will grow from mowing one lawn, to mowing *many* lawns. Soon the Lawnmower Millions will come to life as he hires additional young people into his business. Soon there will be cash flow for purchasing bigger and better equipment. The business will grow, and begin acquiring larger accounts, commercial accounts, requiring more employees and larger equipment purchases. And so on, and so on. The bottom line is this. *"If everybody had to grow up and find a job, there would be no jobs! Somebody, somewhere, has to start a company, first!"*

Consider the stores you shop at every day. The grocery stores, shoe stores, clothing stores, the gas stations and movie theaters. The list could go on and on. Every business you shop at and every business you are employed by was originally started by someone who rose to the challenge of creating their own income. These people are no better or smarter than you are. They are no better or smarter than Rick is, or than your children are at this very moment. The only thing that separates them from a lot of other humans is that they *refused* to give in to the negative pressure that I made people bring into their lives. They were strong enough to remain self-actualized. Some even *re-actualized*.

It is the self-actualized little humans like Rick who are out there working hard and achieving their go-karts that end up creating the jobs that support your mortgage payments and families. Without the Ricks of the world there would be no entrepreneurs. Without entrepreneurs there would be no businesses. Without businesses there would be no jobs.

If everybody had to get a job like everyone else, nobody would be starting their own businesses, and the entire world would be unemployed!

It's true! *Think* about it. Worldwide economic destruction!

Little did you know that a *go-kart* could swing the global economy.

The Thunder Years

Turning the *Blunder Years* into the *Thunder Years* isn't all that compli-cated once you know the logic behind it. It is a logic that has been an under-lying theme in almost everything I have been telling you so far.

The first step to re-actualizing into your *Thunder Years* is accomplished through physical fitness. This is similar to what Maslow would have re-ferred to as your "physical" needs. I *gave* this one to you on a silver platter when I spelled out the "Peanut Butter Fitness Program." Follow this pro-gram and you will be one step closer to home. And by the way, keep in mind that you don't have to necessarily achieve the fitness level of an Olympic athlete, but you do have to make the best with what you have. As you will see, this will become as much a mental attribute as a physical one. You will know what I mean when you get there.

The second step in advancing toward your Thunder Years is hiding in a place you have never looked for it. It's been hiding in your *boredom.* That's right, boredom.

You won't believe this, but boredom was originally brought to earth as a *motivator.* It is a signal that you should be doing something else. Boredom is telling you that you are *capable* of something else. That you are capable of something *more.* But like so many other things, I wrecked that too. Today, boredom doesn't motivate you. Instead, it makes you tired, lazy, and even depressed. In a nutshell, it makes a bad situation, worse!

In some situations, boredom is temporary and shouldn't be worried about. Like sitting in math class when you would rather be playing baseball, or having to attend someone's wedding, when you would rather be bass fishing in your new Ranger bass boat. Boredom has a way of spilling into these kinds of temporary situations, but because they pass so quickly they're not worth changing your life over.

Another place where boredom creeps in is called, "idle time." Most humans consider *idle time* a boring block of time in which there is nothing for them to do.

Whoops.

Bad call.

Idle time is *supposed* to be boring! The *boredom* is supposed to motivate you to begin achieving! Idle time is there so that you *have* the time! Get it? Idle time eliminates your excuse of not *having* the time!

Idle time was designed to be *opportunity* time, but thanks to me it usually becomes *wasted* time.

Some encounters with boredom exist on a very large scale and are designed to mark your path to bigger things. For instance, consider boredom as it relates to your job. *Millions* of you go to work each day to jobs you think are boring. Multiply that number by the forty to fifty hours each week you spend working at those jobs and you will discover that humans are spending *billions* of hours each week feeling bored and unchallenged! *Billions* of hours each week bathing in de-actualization, not recognizing your boredom is a sign that you should be doing something more significant. A signal that you are *capable* of something more significant! Most of you know it! But you fail to react to it.

Do you know that feeling you get that stops you from putting forth the effort to make a change?

I cause that feeling.

Do you know those words you hear that prevent you from taking action?

Those are my words.

Imagine the impact on the world's productivity if every hour spent at a boring job was matched with an hour of studying to achieve a person's *dream* job. Can you imagine what would happen if everyone was working a job, or running a business, that took advantage of their full potential?

YIKES! You would all be rich beyond reason.

Face it, you won't re-actualize into the Thunder Years standing along an assembly line bored to tears, *knowing* that you are capable of more.

Perhaps the character Cole Trickle in the movie, "Days of Thunder" (get the connection there?) was correct when he said, "You have to be good at your job before you can enjoy the rest of your life."

Who says movies don't have their place in reality?

So where do you go from here? You go *inside* yourself.

Eliminating boredom is accomplished by following your own internal excitement and enthusiasm, and then developing it into a sellable abundance of knowledge and expertise.

Sound familiar?

This puts you in the position of earning a living doing something you enjoy. When you are doing something you enjoy it motivates you to do it well, which builds your confidence as well as your career. Doing something well has a natural way of causing your income to rise, helping you to pay for things like a nice house in a safe neighborhood, with good schools for your kids to attend. Your attitude will also become a *successful* attitude, making you more interesting, more attractive and more liked by others. My words here are teaching you how to avoid the paradigm of poverty. I am telling you how to make more money, and I have encouraged you (earlier) to reduce your living expenses. Remember, wearing credit card jewelry does not make you rich and successful. Making *more* money, reducing your debts and expenses and investing the difference, will make you rich and successful. If you are married, follow my advice! You will both argue less about money, your love needs will remain satisfied, and you will retire self-made multi-millionaires. Now *that's* Thunder! And all just because you're bored!

You have just seen the plan to complete the steps of Maslow's Hierarchy. Use Peanut Butter Fitness Program for the first step, and *boredom* to complete the next four!

Follow the advice I am giving you, and in a few short years you might feel good enough to do what the Jeff Gordon website will confirm a man named John did.

Feeling pretty good one day John brought home a go-kart (quarter midget, to be exact) for his 5-year old stepson, Jeff Gordon. Little Jeff appeared to have a knack for driving it. As a matter fact, at age 6 the little guy wanted to race the silly little thing. I did what I could to convince his parents it was a *stupid* idea, and *dangerous* too! But they let him do it anyway. The little rascal ended up winning 35 races that year! Two years later he won the quarter midget national championship at the age of eight! Three years later he branched into go-kart racing. He entered 25 races and won all 25! By age 13, the little guy was driving *650 horsepower* sprint cars!

When Jeff was fourteen, he had his mother drive him to the local Valvoline motor oil distributor in hopes of getting some free motor oil. His mother had to drive, because even though Jeff was driving 650 horsepower sprint cars, he wasn't old enough to have his driver's license!

Jeff kept racing his way up through the ranks, and in 1993 he was awarded Winston Cup Rookie of the Year honors. He continued racing and winning, and in 1998 generated an amazing $8,300,000.00 from endorsements and licensing, another $1,500,000.00 as a salary, and won another $8,200,000.00 in prize money!

Did you follow that? That is *eighteen million dollars* in one year!

This is what can happen when happy-to-be-alive, self-actualized parents raise and encourage self-actualized children. They have *fun* together. They allow each other to pursue their *own* enthusiasm. They don't *judge* each other's goals, they *encourage* each other's goals!

What's it like in your house? What would happen if your son or daughter told you they wanted to be a professional athlete? Would you give them my "Do you know the odds of making it?" speech, and talk them into doing what *you* think is important? Or would you drive them to the local Valvoline oil distributor like Jeff Gordon's mom did for Jeff?

Professional athletes are great examples of poor listeners. If they weren't, they could all be enjoying exciting pizza delivery jobs right now!

Sexual Synergy

Synergy occurs when the *total* of something becomes greater than the sum of its individual parts. Sexual synergy, while it isn't specifically goal oriented like other forms of synergy, works something like this:

Two teenaged boys are outside running after school. The brisk running pace they had enjoyed earlier has slowed to a laborious jog as they enter their fifth mile. The exhausting 91-degree temperature is taking its toll. Their mouths are dry, their shoulders are rounded and their legs have become heavy. Completing another mile is beginning to seem impossible, but that is when it happens. The boys see two very shapely teenaged girls in bikinis in the front yard of the house up ahead. The girls are unfolding beach towels across the plush green lawn, obviously hoping to spend some time in the warm afternoon sun.

Instantly, the boy's energy levels begin to rise. Their rounded shoulders pull back straight, their chins come up, their chests come out and their tired legs become feather light. The exhausted boys of just a moment ago now find themselves sprinting past the girls in an effortless *blur* of speed. This is *sexual synergy* in its earliest form.

Here is a piece of advice for athletic coaches. If you want to see harder hitting, faster running, and higher scoring in the next big game, you need to consider a new intangible. You need to know which of your players have cheering girlfriends in the stands. Because love conquers all... including opposing teams!

Sexual synergy is an inherent, primal source of raw energy and strength. It was created to exist in abundance and *not* be suppressed, although I was certainly able to get some of you to try.

For instance, let's talk about some of the men out there.

To understand the success I had at getting the human male to misunderstand the productive value of sexual synergy, you need to go all the way back to the days of Susan B. Anthony. Most of you know Susan B. Anthony as an advocate for women's rights, but there was a side to Suzy (that's what we call her here) that you probably aren't aware of. Aside from being one of the original Mothers of America, Susan B. Anthony was also a *convicted criminal*. That's right, she was an ex-con! Since you probably didn't know that, then you probably don't know what she was arrested for, either.

Susan B. Anthony was charged and convicted for the crime of...

(Drum roll please)

Voting for President!

That's no joke! By the time I had finished with the lawmakers of those days it had actually become a criminal for a woman to vote in a presidential election. If she did, she went to jail.

Can you believe that? To better understand the level of success I had with these men you need to examine the very Bible they believed in. Try not to forget that these are the same men who went as far as to place the words, "In God We Trust" throughout the significant buildings of Washington, D.C., as well as on all of their money. Those words are still there on your money today!

According to the book of Genesis in their Bible, God made man and named the first one, Adam. After a short time Adam became lonely, causing God to determine that it was not good for man to be alone. God thought about it, and decided to make a companion for Adam.

One at time God began creating various living creatures for Adam to spend time with, but none of them seemed to please Adam for any length of time. I wasn't around back then, but as the story goes, Adam apparently had God pretty well stumped. He had God pacing around deep in thought, thumb under his chin, index finger tapping against his lips, "How about a cow!" God would exclaim.

ZAP! Adam was given a cow. It was okay for a while, but soon Adam needed more.

God went back to his pondering.

"How about a horse!"

ZAP! Adam had a horse. It too was okay for a while, and fun to ride on, but still Adam needed more.

"How about a cat!"

ZAP! Adam had a cat. "Yuck!" (A total disaster.)

This went on and on until one day God finally had an idea. God made Adam sleep, and while he was asleep, God removed one of Adams ribs and from it he created woman.

If you're a woman and the thought of that makes you scoff and roll your eyes, try not to be too upset. You can blame me for the men who think the rib thing gives them some kind of mythical superiority. **The fact is, it took the creation of woman to finally rev Adam's engine, and without that, the human male would not have survived.** Not physically, or even emotionally. That makes woman a man's most vitally important companion. A concept certain men, thanks to me, have failed to catch on to. That made it easy for me to get some women involved in a few anti-synergy tricks of their own. For instance, because men are such *visual* creatures and can experience very high levels of energy while in the presence of a beautiful woman, I decided to launch a "Looks aren't important" campaign. Almost everyone has heard this at one time or another. Trying to get women to give up on looking beautiful would rob men of the synergistic energy they feel when they are around them. Fewer beautiful women, fewer wildly productive bursts of energy. Little girls would no longer make little boys run faster.

Some of you bought into this, but only for a while. Humans began to realize that successful relationships are the result of a mixture of attributes. Attributes like personality, honesty, trustworthiness, marital history, religious beliefs, common interests, and physical appearance are all important and all carry value. A person looking to build a successful relationship may find someone who has attributes that are weak in some areas, but very strong in others. In the end, the total of all of a person's attributes, as if they are a part of a mathematical formula, either create a chemistry that causes one person to become attracted to another, or it doesn't.

Selectively eliminating a specific attribute such as a person's appearance and believing it doesn't affect the quality of a relationship is a testimony to the quality of my work. This can be proven quite easily. For example, just try *changing* the attribute. Try selecting *personality,* or *honesty,* and disregarding it the same way some of you have tried to disregard personal appearance. How would you react to someone who told you this:

"When it comes to relationships *honesty* doesn't matter. Go ahead and lie, it isn't a big deal."

In the end, my "Looks don't matter" campaign failed miserably. Woman and men alike continue to spend billions of dollars each year on clothes, jewelry, hair care and fitness, all in an effort to improve and maintain their physical appearance.

When you look better, you feel better. When a person feels better, they beome more productive and more fun for others to spend time with! Granted, a person's appearance cannot sustain a relationship, and people work on their fitness and appearance for more than one reason. But to selectively disregard the importance of any given relationship attribute shows a lack of understanding of how all of the attributes work together to create a *successful* relationship. Not understanding this is a sad thing, because a quality, loving relationship between a man and a woman is a remarkably powerful creation. More powerful than anything you can create on your own.

No Guts, No Gloria

My next attempt to suppress sexual synergy was another total disaster. Since I couldn't stop women from wanting to be beautiful, I had to try something else to stop little girls from making little boys run faster. That is when I created something called the "Feminist" movement. Remember? The burning-of-the-bra that caused a sexual earthquake?

My hope for the feminist movement was built upon a newly created *adversarial* element. Like making women *glare* at men who held a door for them… that kind of thing. If you are a man who dated his way through the 1980's you know exactly what I'm talking about. I also made an effort to confuse being "equal" with trying to become "identical." Like when I tried to make women feel the need to wear pinstriped suits, with *pants!*

A relatively short-lived fashion snafu.

Unfortunately, I had to pull the plug on the whole idea. Please understand that my intentions with feminism were aimed strictly at adults, but before long parents had started dragging their kids into it! Parents began filing lawsuits to get their little boys into Girl Scouts, or to get their little girls into Boys Scouts. (Keep in mind that this is not the same as when a girl wants to play hockey and there is only *one* team, a *boy's* team to play on.)

While all of these lawsuits gave me some interesting ideas about suppressing the economy (which you'll read about later) my intention was never to cause irreversible embarrassment to little humans! After the parents of these children had finished publicly embarrassing their kids, they quickly brushed them aside to rental parents (day care) so as to resume their high profile careers at the local *Budget Clips*. Real nice job with the priorities.

Kids are little adults, not pawns to be used on the feminism chessboard!

Luckily, about all that's left of my feminist movement are some bits and pieces called, "Unisex." You still see some of this on bathroom doors and occasionally even on some clothing racks. But come on, Unisex? When you stop and think about it, what could possibly be the long-term mission of a "Unisex" movement? To create a single-sex species that cannot reproduce? You would have an entire world of "Pats" running around ultimately leading to the extinction of the human race!

The next time you see a Unisex sign on the door of a public bathroom, take it down and bring it in there with you. What you do with it after that is up to you.

The reality of the sexes is that men and woman are in this life together. You are by design genetically *dependent* upon each other. How much *more* equal can two humans be than two humans who are made from the same blood, bone, and DNA? Besides that, you would both perish without each other!

Wouldn't life be more enjoyable if you could both *celebrate* your differences? Shouldn't men be allowed to be masculine, and still be respected by women as their equal? Shouldn't women be allowed to be feminine, and still be respected by men as *their* equal? Accepting this breathes life into the deepest levels of mutual respect, ultimately allowing the most productive levels of synergy to occur.

When the sexes respect each other for who they are, they discover reservoirs of unparalleled creativity, power and courage. A sexual chemistry, a sexual *synergy* that makes each of you better than you could ever be by yourself. Every teenaged boy knows this, as does every self-made million-aire.

Check the Ford Motor Company's website, and turn the calendar back to July 30, 1863. It was on that day in the town now called Dearborn, Michigan, that William and Mary Ford gave birth to the first of their six children. It was a son named, Henry.

As a child Henry had no special advantages. He spent his days attending school in a one-room schoolhouse and doing chores on the family farm. Henry didn't really enjoy farm life, but he did like working on mechanical things.

At the age of sixteen, Henry left home and moved to Detroit to work as an apprentice machinist. A few years later he returned to Dearborn, working in factories, overhauling his family's farm equipment, and occasionally helping out as a farm hand. Not exactly a glamorous living but it paid the bills. A few years later he met Clara Bryant, the woman whose love would provide Henry with the power to change the course of history.

Henry and Clara were married in 1888. He was working at a sawmill at the time, but would soon become an engineer at the Edison Illuminating Company. (Edison... another bad listener.) When Henry was promoted to Edison's Chief Engineer, it provided him with both the time and money to begin experimenting with internal combustion engines, which is the same operating principle that still powers your automobiles today.

In 1896 Henry completed a four-wheeled self-propelled vehicle called the Quadricycle, and then set his sights on producing automobiles.

Henry's first attempt to create an automobile manufacturing company ended in failure. He regrouped and tried again, but his second attempt also ended failure.

Henry was determined. He tried a third time and in 1903 the Ford Motor Company was created. A short time later Henry's now famous "Model T" had made the Ford Motor Company the largest automobile manufacturing company in the world.

Henry Ford was an amazing man who came from common roots and made it to the top of his field. Ironically, he didn't attribute his success to long hours of scheduling in a fashionable, leather-bound planner. Nor did he attribute his success to the changing his "paradigm."

He had never heard of either of these.

Henry Ford attributed his ability to succeed to the love and support of his wife, Clara. Henry believed that, "Behind every successful man is a successful woman." He knew that little girls could make little boys run faster, and that a good woman could make a good man, *rich.* He's not alone.

In the summer of 2000, the richest man in the world, Bill Gates, was interviewed on national television. **The interviewer reviewed the accumulation of all of Bill's wealth, and then asked Bill what he considered to be the most valuable asset to his success. Bill's eyes began to tear, his lips gently quivered, and in a soft voice he replied, "The love of my wife."**

"Frivolous" is my Middle Name

Magnum P.I. was a good name for a TV show about a private investigator, but it works even better as a title for what I have caused the *personal injury* system to do to your economy. The title, "Magnum Personal Injury" probably strikes a little closer to home.

As you know, big goals often require a sizeable sum of money to pursue. If you are like most people, that money has to come straight out of your *spendable* household income. Elevating the personal injury system to the level it is at today consumes your spendable household income, straining your financial ability to pursue those goals. For example, the auto industry recently reported that in the same amount of time it took for the cost of producing an automobile to *double*, your cost to actually purchase the car had risen *five times* that cost! They regretfully sighted the cost of *liability* as the reason for these magnificent expenses. In other words, if it wasn't for the number of personal injury lawsuits, many of them frivolous, being filed against the automobile companies, the cost of a new car would be a fraction of what it is today, leaving more of your goal-chasing spendable income intact.

Liability expenses also show up in the cost of your insurance premiums. One driver bumps into another car and before you can blink there is a frivolous lawsuit filed for whiplash, lost wages and emotional suffering (that is of course, while the injured driver is not out playing golf).

Do you know who pays the cost of all of those lawsuit settlements? You do. Every product you purchase and every insurance premium you pay is loaded with additional dollars to cover these costs. Basically, every person who is suing someone in an effort to make a quick buck isn't just suing the person named in the lawsuit. They are also suing you, and everyone else you know, because every one of you is paying their settlement dollars through the cost of ever rising insurance premiums.

It's easy to determine when I've gotten someone to file a personal injury lawsuit with the intent of making some easy money. Midway through the tennis match that you will both be playing in (magically, playing tennis does not seem to aggravate the pain they have been suffering) they will say to you, "Besides, I'm really not suing the other driver. I'm really only suing their insurance company."

Get out your checkbook.

Since I have caused so much money to flow *out* of your household, it only seems fair that I tell you a few ways to keep some money *in* your household.

Since we have been talking about expenses associated with the auto industry, let's stay on that theme. I am going to give you and the car companies a way to significantly reduce the cost of a new automobile. Then I will tell you how to eliminate frivolous personal injury lawsuits altogether. This will relieve the congestion in the court system, allowing it to concentrate on legitimate court cases.

Reducing the amount of liability dollars built into the price of new cars will make them much more affordable to everyone. More importantly, this will allow more of your hard earned dollars to stay at home where they belong, putting you in a better financial position to pursue your goals.

As we work to reduce the cost of your next new car, I hope you won't mind, but I would like to get the folks at Pontiac Motors involved with this. I feel a little obligated here. Not long ago some of the other spirits and I had an ugly car contest. In order to win the contest we not only had to design the ugliest car, but then we had influence one of the car companies to actually build it!

I won!

A short time later my winning design hit the road. You won't believe it, but the Pontiac Aztec was all my idea! Now you know why I owe Pontiac a favor.

By the way, I was also the spirit behind some other products you might remember. Like the New COKE of the 80's, or Miller Clear Beer in the 90's, but those are entirely different stories.

Okay Pontiac, it is time to make amends. Select one of the cars in your line. Let's say, the Grand Prix. How would you like to shatter every sales record known to your industry? **Then don't make any changes to this car for a three-year period.** In other words, once you have created the next new model year of the already sporty Grand Prix, instead of spending millions of dollars on Research & Development each year for the remaining two years (which you will have to recoup in the sticker price), don't spend any! Changes are expensive! Not making any to the new Pontiac Grand Prix will *drastically* reduce the sticker price, making it a brand new car that is affordable to everyone. Your Pubic Relations people will go crazy for the publicity this will generate, and keep in mind that publicity historically out-pulls advertising *six-to-one*, and it is free!

I know what you are thinking. You are thinking that the car won't sell because consumers always want to have the latest and greatest. You are also thinking that consumers won't buy a new car that is already three model years old. But you are wrong. First of all, the car will be so affordable that many consumers will not be able to resist it. Secondly, even in the car's third year, it is not as though the consumer is buying a car that has been sitting on the lot for three years. The consumer will be buying a new car that is fresh off the assembly line! It will be a brand new, clean, zero miles new car with a full warranty and best of all, that new car smell! All for a fraction of what a new car would normally cost. The final kicker is this. You don't have to market the car as though it will be hanging around for three more years. You market the vehicle as a car that has come out three years early! In other words, in the year 2004, you don't present the car as a 2004 Pontiac Grand Prix that is going to be unchanged for the next three years. In the year 2004, you present the 2007 Pontiac Grand Prix that is hitting the market three years early! That means in 2007 it will still be in its current model year!

I am expecting a heavy commission for this one.

How Much For That Lawsuit

In The Window?

I didn't create the personal injury system, but I did help it out a little. Do you know all of those personal injury commercials you keep seeing on television? They are the commercials where a lawyer says, "We don't charge a fee until we collect a settlement for you." Did you know those commercials used to be illegal? Well, they were. But I changed all that. Today those commercials are not only legal, but they have produced personal injury lawsuits in record numbers, and not just related to the auto industry.

Let's say you are the owner of a nice suburban home. It is a tan two-story colonial with a three-car garage, a large green lawn and a beautiful garden in the back yard. You even have a dog. A good natured Black Labrador, female. You also have some pretty good neighbors, who coincidentally, have a couple of children about the same ages of your own children.

This should sound pretty good so far, but let's put a few things in motion.

It is Friday night. Your neighbor's teenaged boy, who has just been given a full basketball scholarship for next year at the local university, is out with some friends. Feeling a little up-to-no-good, they sneak into your garden and steal some tomatoes to throw at passing automobiles. The boys stand in the dark between the two houses, quietly waiting for a car to drive by. It takes only a minute, and through the darkness shine the headlight beams of an approaching automobile. The boys patiently take aim, and at just the right moment, tomatoes away!

Bang! Bang. **BANG!**

The boy's giggles are quickly drowned out by the sound of tires squealing to a stop. They hear a car door open, and then a second door, and then a third! To the boy's dismay the driver of the automobile was not alone in the car, and even more terrifying is the fact that the driver and all of his buddies are now running straight towards them! Your neighbor's boy and his friends take off running through your back yard. Unfortunately, your neighbor's son trips on the stake that is screwed into the ground that anchors your dog's leash. He falls to the ground, breaking the wrist of his right arm.

About this time, you switch on the back yard light to see what all the commotion is about. You open your back door and find your neighbor's son lying on your property, badly injured.

Your neighbor, angry at his son and even feeling a little embarrassed, happens to watch a television commercial that begins with the words, "Have you or anyone you know been injured?" He then hears the words, "We don't charge a fee until we collect money for you."

A few weeks later you receive a letter from Heckel, Jeckel, Whizbang & Fontz, Attorneys at Law, informing you that you are being sued for $1,000,000.00.

The lawsuit is claiming negligence on your part for not having a "No Trespassing" sign in your yard; for your garden not having an electrically charged six-foot tall cyclone fence with barbed wire top; for your backyard not being lit with 25-billion candle power stadium lighting at night; for not having a large red flag attached to the dog stake; and for not having a sign next to the dog stake that reads, "Watch your step." The lawsuit is also claiming the break to the boy's right arm has suspended his basketball scholarship, and potentially destroyed his career in the NBA.

Because you are being sued for an amount greater than what is covered under your homeowner's insurance policy, you hire an attorney. This immediately begins costing *you* money. Your homeowner's insurance company also gets an attorney involved, who makes an assessment of the case. He determines that, win or lose, it will cost at least $35,000.00 to bring the case to trial. He advises his company (your insurance company) to offer your neighbor $25,000.00 just to make it go away.

This becomes free money for your neighbor and his attorney. All they had to do was file the lawsuit and they automatically received a $25,0000.00 settlement offer from your insurance company, because it will cost them *more* money to bring it to trial. For the insurance company it is a Catch 22. For your neighbor and his personal injury lawyer, it is a license to steal.

Unfortunately for you and everyone else, just like so many other liability expenses, the cost of these bogus lawsuits and subsequent settlement dollars come straight out of your household income every time you pay your ever increasing homeowners insurance premiums.

Perhaps you should cut your insurance company a little slack next time you see the size of your premiums. Instead, try blaming me. You can also blame the humans, and the personal injury lawyers, who are intentionally taking advantage of the legal system and slowly bleeding you out of your dream-chasing spendable dollars.

When you think about it, the Personal Injury system is pretty amazing. It allows someone to sue you without risking one dime of their own money. The insurance companies are often forced to issue settlement dollars because it is less expensive than fighting. The suing attorney takes a percentage of the settlement dollars and the person suing you keeps the rest! They sue you for free and get money for doing it! Meanwhile, you are forced to hire an attorney, which will cost you big money, and you may have done nothing wrong!

However, since there are options to all of this, let's play out our example and see what the neighbor does.

Option #1. Your neighbor accepts the $25,000.00 settlement. He gives his attorney the typical one third ($7,500.00), and then bankrolls the remaining $17,500.00. Pure profit for having a punk kid hit a car with one of your tomatoes. Meanwhile, you get stuck paying your own legal bill, and everyone else's insurance bills increase.

Option #2. Your neighbor does not take the money. He and his attorney turn down the $25,000.00, and then turn down a $35,000.00 offer. They want the full $1,000,000.00. A few months later, deep into the trial, they find out they blew it! The court decides your neighbor's lawsuit is ridiculous. The judge warns his attorney for bringing such a case, and then throws the entire case out of court. Your neighbor doesn't collect a dime! But he also didn't incur any legal expenses because his attorney was basing his fee on settlement dollars.

But let's talk about you.

Your attorney's fees have now amassed to nearly $35,000.00, none of which are covered by insurance!

To make sure we are clear about this, here are the events that occurred in our example. While sitting alone watching television on a Friday night your neighbor's kid stole a tomato out of your garden and threw it at a car. It cost his father *nothing* to sue you, but it is going to cost you $35,000.00 even though you won!

What do you think?

Hey, don't blame me. I didn't create the system, all I did was make it worse. But just as I did with the price of new automobiles, I'll tell you how to fix this system also. In fact, I can tell you how to fix it in two simple words.

"Loser pays."

If you want to fix the personal injury system and start bringing the cost of goods and services back in line, obligate the plaintiff (the person actually filing the lawsuit) to a *Loser Pays* system. **With the Loser Pays system, if someone sues you and *they lose,* they are obligated to pay all of *your* attorney fees!** That means that if you are brought to court by way of a lawsuit, and the judge determines it is frivolous, you walk away clean.

Do you really think someone would sue you if there was a chance it will end up *costing* them money?

In other words, if your neighbor's son hits a car with a tomato and gets hurt in your yard while running away from the driver, do you really believe his father would sue you if it might cost him several thousand dollars if he loses?

With a Loser Pays system you would find that many of the drivers out there crying "whiplash" would start realizing that their necks don't feel so bad after all.

Something else that could happen in the meantime, is the policing of lawyers by other lawyers. Let's face it, hard working professional lawyers have seen the reputation of their prestigious profession destroyed by personal injury lawyers abusing a system that was designed to compensate people who have truly suffered a loss.

As a human you have to accept that there are accidents in your world. They can happen to anyone, and be caused by anyone. Even you. They are an unfortunate part of life. There are also acts of negligence that occur. I refer to acts of negligence as, "negligents." There is a big difference between an "accident" and a "negligent," particularly with respect to "intent of doing harm." Recognizing this difference will determine whether you should consider suing your neighbor, or *grounding your kid,* and then visiting your neighbor with a cold beer and a store bought tomato to replace the one that is now missing.

When the personal injury system becomes a Loser Pays system, humans will stop suing each other and start playing together again. Fathers will no longer be afraid to coach Little League, and will be down at the park tossing baseballs around. Doctors will once again visit with pregnant mothers without fear of losing their practice.

More people will be having folks over for barbecues.

Being friendly and sociable is not only an asset, it is a part of your nature. But then again, it always seems to take a tragedy for some of you to realize that.

It shouldn't take the threat of raging floodwaters, the devastation of a tornado, or a terrorist attack to bring out the best in people!

Why should it take a crisis for the people of a neighborhood, or a country, to come together?

Little did you realize how offering a neighbor a cold beer and a piece of chicken can help reduce the sticker price of a new automobile, improve the efficiency of the legal system, and leave you better prepared next time a raging storm approaches. It will also keep more goal-chasing dollars in your pocket, and that can be the thing that dreams are made of.

Greed is a bad thing, so spread love, not law.

Got, Fear?

Conquering your fear can be a productive accomplishment. Like conquering the fear you might have just before competing in a major sports event, or as you are stepping up to speak before a large group of people. But conquering fear, and not having any fear, can be completely different things. For example, when a criminal engages in illegal activity because they have no fear of the legal system. This would all change with the demise of frivolous lawsuits, as your court system would once again have the time to concentrate on the things they really need to. Like actually *prosecuting* criminals, for example. Of course, taking criminals off the streets of your neighborhood might require funding a few more prisons, and we wouldn't want to jeopardize any of that new baseball stadium money...

A number of your weakest humans have tried to make you believe that no one is responsible for their behavior anymore. Unfortunately, when you get where I am now, trying to blame bad behavior on something like a television show isn't considered a valid excuse. If you screw up here, you get punished accordingly.

Imagine that... *accountability.*

The thought of getting punished in the spiritual world might catch some of you off guard, but one of the most amazing things you will discover when you get here is that life in the spiritual world is remarkably similar to life on earth, only on a much grander scale. For example, some of the places you can live here are unbelievably nice, but only if you play your cards right while you are still living on earth. That might be a difficult concept to accept, but why else do you suppose you were put where you are? Why would you be placed on earth, judged for how you lived, and then be sent for eternity to someplace completely different? Does a parent send a child to summer gymnastics camp with the intent of putting the child in chess club? Does an automotive repair shop send its mechanics to repair school so after they return they can go to work as web-page designers?

No!

You are on earth today being trained and evaluated for how well you will do when you get to where I am today. And when it comes to behavior, accountability and discipline, the world better start getting its act together. As time has been passing some of your undisciplined earthlings have begun showing up here, and quite honestly, they can be a real pain in the spiritual neck.

Perhaps I should point the finger of blame at myself. As you know, I thought I could have a little fun suppressing your household economics through bogus "whiplash" lawsuits and that kind of thing. But just like some of my other mischief, I never dreamed it would eventually interfere with the healthy development of little humans. For instance, do you know why students have such little fear of teachers or principals? Or why so many children have such little fear of their parents? It's because the teachers and parents, the *adults,* are afraid of being sued for issuing discipline!

Maybe my proposed changes to your legal system will do more than just lower your cost of living. Perhaps it will put discipline back into your lives, because there are very few fifteen-year olds who will sue their parents, and very few parents who will sue teachers, knowing that it might cost them several thousand dollars if they don't really have a legitimate reason for doing so!

Not long ago, before kids brought bombs and guns to school, parents felt it was necessary to raise their own children. They disciplined them in different ways based on what worked best in getting the child to respond. For example, when some kids got into trouble their parents responded by giving them the *silent treatment*. For the softer hearted kids, this was the worst punishment imaginable. It would generate terrible suffering, causing them to change their behavior in order to return to their parent's good graces.

Then there were other kids who needed something more. Like being scolded, or grounded. This was something similar to what parents today call, *Time Out*. For these kids, the loss of their freedom was an intense penalty, and would cause them to rethink their behavior.

Finally, there were other, more aggressive kids. For them the silent treatment it was actually a bonus! Water off a duck's back. Parents tried grounding these kids, but that just made them sneak out their windows. That's when these kids finally got a good old-fashioned swat across the britches from dear ol' dad. *Ouch!*

That finally got their attention. But for those of you who believe that type of thing is out of line, here is a piece of logic for you to ponder.

Have you ever been in need of money? Of course you have. So why didn't you rob a bank?

Because you knew that it was wrong? Correct? You also knew that if you got caught you would go to jail for a very long time and you didn't want that to happen.

But suppose the penalty for robbing a bank wasn't so bad? Suppose the penalty was only a $10,000.00 fine? Then would you try it? Or better yet, suppose it was only a $1,000.00 fine? Then would you?

Suppose it was only a $100.00 fine?

135

Suppose it was only a $10.00 fine?

Ask yourself, if you desperately needed money and the penalty for robbing a bank, should you get caught, was only a $10.00 fine? Would you *maybe* consider trying it?

Now you know one of the differences between you and a person who robs banks. They are no more afraid of going to jail for a few years then you are of paying a ten-dollar fine, so when they get tempted, they try it. But suppose the penalty for robbing a bank was a *mandatory* life sentence?

Suddenly you would have fewer people trying to rob banks.

And that's exactly why some kids straighten out from the silent treatment, and other kids eventually need to get their fannies whacked.

Hall of Fame football coach, Vince Lombardi said, "If you treat everyone the same, you mistreat all but one person." Perhaps that applies to more than just football.

Do you know why living in a disciplined environment is so important for younger humans? It is because discipline is about *accountability*. It is about accepting responsibility, which leads to *taking* responsibility! And not just for their problems, but for their future.

Great leaders are developed upon a foundation of discipline. Every young human deserves this chance. By not providing it, the world is doing its children a disservice, because well disciplined individuals are more likely to take charge of their life and *make* their dreams happen, as opposed to aimlessly wondering around expecting things to be handed to them. There are some who will disagree with me on this, but those are the same folks who think that a $10,000.00 fine for robbing a bank shows discrimination against the poor.

Hold yourself accountable, even if no one else will.

Shooting Down Leadership

and Responsibility

Squeaky humans (adults who live to complain) have a way of catching the ear of the media, and when that happens I have ensured that, right or wrong, public opinion tends to swing toward the squeak. Developing into a great leader means knowing that just because something is a headline in the morning paper doesn't mean it is right, or that you must disregard your own thoughts on the issue. This is a classic example of learning all that you can, but *remembering the privilege of thinking for yourself.*

You don't have to throw in the intellectual towel just because there is a new wave of public opinion!

I also enjoy provoking a good shouting match, but great leaders are able to seek out and discuss multiple aspects of the most controversial of issues, and do so without breaking into temper flaring arguments. They know that when it comes to sensitive discussions, as volume increases, the ability to clearly explore all sides of an issue begins to end.

For example, one of your most hotly contested and controversial issues is the firearm (handgun) issue. There is an effort (and let's be sure to get this straight), to swing public opinion into allowing violent criminals to escape responsibility by blaming a mechanical object for a human action?

You *must* be kidding, but let's all try to stay calm.

Have you ever stopped to consider that if you can blame a mechanical object for a human action, then you can also blame a mechanical object for a lack of human action? If that is the logic you are buying into, then nobody will ever have to take responsibility for anything ever again. Not for their success, and not for their lack of it. Soon, things will sound something like this:

"Our daughter Tammy could have been an Olympic gymnast, but her stupid bicycle didn't like her so it broke down on purpose. After that she never made it to another day of gymnastics. That darn bicycle ruined our daughter's Olympic hopes."

Kiss *leadership* goodbye. They could have gotten the bicycle repaired. They could have bought her a new bicycle. Tammy could have taken the bus, or they could have driven her. But noooooooooo, blame it on the bicycle and live a life of excuses.

Don't laugh, because unless you are careful, that's where some of today's logic will take you. That is why so many people on earth are focusing their attention on controlling inanimate objects, when they actually need to be trying to control *humans*.

Sorry, but sometimes the truth hurts.

Just to be clear, nothing is being advocated here. The firearm issue is a large onion with many layers needing to be peeled. Here are just a few.

Firearms expose ignorance, bring unfair advantages to the weak, can be used as instruments to harm living things, and make hypocrites out of otherwise intelligent humans.

Regarding guns exposing ignorance. Most of the people who want guns removed from society either do not currently own a gun, have *never* owned a gun, or have never attended any type of gun safety training or education. These are usually the same people who are convinced that guns have the capacity to demonstrate *emotion*. That guns can actually become angry to the point of being violent! They obviously believe this, because they keep using the term, "gun violence."

So can a gun also become pleasant and cheerful?

This is an example of what can happen when you remove human discipline and responsibility from your society.

How silly can it get? "Why, our little Billy didn't shoot that other little boy. It was that darn pistol. You were a *bad* little pistol today. Bad. Bad. Bad."

Do humans come home after work and say things like, "Hi honey, I'm home. How are things around house?"

"Well dear, Billy is upstairs doing his homework, but you'll have to have another talk with that pistol of yours. While I was at the store it pee'd in the kitchen, pooped on the carpet, chewed up a shoe and bit the mailman."

These are the same people who blame their children's violence on the television and music and industries. Listen, everybody knows that television and music doesn't have to contain the content that some of it does, but parents could also be teaching their children not to pay attention to it.

Of course, parents would probably have to be at home raising their own children to do that...

There is even more bad news. Back in the 1960's almost every toy box was filled with toy guns of all types. Army rifles and pistols. Cowboy rifles and pistols. There were rubber knives for scalping the white man, and if you were really lucky, the Johnny Seven O.M.A.. The Johnny Seven had *seven guns in one!* Including a missile launcher, grenade launcher and detachable pistol. Kids everywhere were running around shooting each other with plastic bullets, yelling things like, "You're dead, I shot you!" When they weren't outside shooting guns at each other, they were inside watching television shows about cowboys shooting Indians, and Indians scalping cowboys. They were also watching army shows like Combat, and Rat Patrol, that were full of gunfire and people dying. Yet, many humans believe that today's television shows and video games are *more* violent? More sexual, absolutely. But when it comes to comparing violent environments, perhaps you should try reversing the timetables.

Suppose the kids in the 1960's only played video games the way kids do today, and kids of today played with toy guns the way kids played back then? Then do you know what you would be hearing people say about the cause of "gun" violence? It would sound something like this:

"Just look at what's happened. Why, back in the 1960's our kids were only exposed to guns and violence in music and video games. Today they have progressed to *acting out* their violence! They are actually running around shooting each other with plastic bullets! And have you seen that Johnny Seven O.M.A.? It can kill someone in seven different ways! It even has a grenade launcher! We need to get back to the good old days when our children only listened to music and played video games!"

How many times in the 1960's, when little humans played with toy guns every day, did a student go on a shooting rampage at his or her school?

Why didn't every World War II veteran eventually go postal?

Because people that were raised in disciplined generations have a more clear understanding of right and wrong. They are more willing to accept the responsibility of their actions, and they have more respect for authority.

Your society today may not have a problem with "gun" violence after all. It may be having a problem with "human" violence, and you can put it to the test quite easily. Just try something *accountable,* like making the carrying of a firearm without a permit a mandatory ten-year prison sentence. Period. No plea-bargains. No more 3-hots and a cot, and back on the streets the next day. *Ten years.* This will tell the story.

Try it, and watch how quickly your guns begin improving their behavior.

None of this means that people shouldn't have guns, it just means they have to raise *responsible* guns. Either way, there is a good chance that a ten-year penalty (a ten-year fanny whacking) will put a dent in the problem.

If you are one of the humans who think society would be safer if the government took away all of the guns, I might suggest we put your logic to the test. If your logic is sound and consistent, then you should also agree that the government should take away everyone's cars, also. If mechanical objects are really the problem, then statistically speaking, "car violence" kills more people than guns do. Therefore, cars should be taken away first!

"Violent cars are killing too many people. Turn over your keys."

Now you know how law abiding gun owners feel.

When it comes to violence, a gun in the house is about as dangerous as a shovel in the garage. When I lived on earth I had as many as twenty-four different firearms during the course of my lifetime, and they were all very well behaved. But then again so were my shovels. Maybe that's because they were raised in an educated and disciplined household.

Another one of the misunderstood elements of guns is how they bring unfair advantages to the weak. For example, a rather large man is awakened at night to find a teenaged thief is holding him at gunpoint. The man angrily tells the thief, "You little punk. How dare you threaten me in my own house. If you didn't have that gun I'd tear you apart."

While having a gun clearly creates an unfair advantage to the thief, having a gun will also turn the homeowner into a hypocrite, and here's how.

That very next weekend the homeowner loads a high-powered rifle and goes into the woods on a bear hunt. When he finally corners a bear, the bear looks at him and thinks to itself, "You little punk. How dare you threaten me in my own house. If you didn't have that gun I'd tear you apart." Just then the homeowner, in the ultimate act of hypocrisy, pulls the trigger and, "click." A misfire! And so the bear ate him, enjoying his meal with a fine bottle of Chianti.

I have no problem with that. It was a fair fight. As a matter fact, if you, yourself, want to go bear hunting I say have at it. Get in there big fella. Unless of course you are planning to bear hunt like a weenie and use a rifle. If that's the case...

"Attention All Animal Lovers! The next time you hear the D.N.R. is issuing bear hunting permits, get out and buy up as many as you can!"

That way there won't be any left for those folks carrying rifles. Get it?

Oh, and by the way. I hear deer hunting can also be a lot of fun, but you'll have to be fairly swift on your feet to catch one. (It sucks being in a fair fight, doesn't it?)

If there is any single argument for gun ownership, it is the most grand and obvious argument of all.

Let me ask you this, "Do you feel safe living in the United States?"

The obvious answer is, yes. Do you know why you feel safe? It is because the United States has the strongest military in the world, particularly when it comes time to defense! The United States is extremely capable of defending itself against aggressive attacks. Other countries know that if they attempt to do harm against your country, they will suffer terrible consequences.

If you examine that logic and attach the test of consistency to it, then a heavily defended home should be better protected from aggressors who attempt to enter and cause harm to you and your family. That doesn't suggest people should be walking around in grocery stores heavily armed and looking for trouble, but at the same time, a law-abiding homeowner should be allowed to protect his or her home and family. It is a system that works at the national level, and one that will also work at the neighborhood level. If you don't accept that, just ask yourself how safe you would feel living in the United States if it decided to do away with its military? How do you suppose some aggressive other countries might behave if they knew the United States was no longer defending itself?

Perhaps it is time to stop all of the inconsistent infighting and reexamine the roadmap that was left for you by your Founding Fathers. After all, your country is also *their* country, you realize. The Pledge of Allegiance, while all but forgotten until a terrorist attack, is the most profound mission statement of all time. It calls for "One nation under God," giving your country a common moral beacon. It calls for your country to be "indivisible," which gives you strength against aggressive other nations. It also calls for "Liberty and *Justice* for all."

It is quite obvious that the squeaky humans want their free run of liberties and freedoms, but their general reluctance towards *justice* is alarming.

Justice is a powerful event. It is a magnificent leadership tool. Justice is about *fairness and accountability,* and yes, can even involve punishment for a person's illegal actions!

It would appear that if you want guns to stop chewing on shoes and biting the mailman, perhaps you should seek a little guidance from your Founding Fathers. They weren't perfect, but they were trying their best to create the finest and safest country possible for you and your family to live in. If you listen very carefully, you may even hear them calling to you right now.

Shhhhhhhhh. Listen...

Hear that?

Great leaders do not fear difficult issues.

High Performance Corporate Behavior

Before finishing up and actually *proving* the existence of God, I have a few chapters on business, and a few more words on leadership, that you *and your bosses* may want to ponder.

Whether you are young and still in school, a current member of the working force, or are at the top of your executive game, the following pages will approach corporate performance in ways that cannot be found in any formal school curriculum. Probably because there aren't any schools that would hire something like myself as a professor. But if you want to make huge impacts in the career field for which you are headed, or maximize the potential of the company you are currently working for, you will find the following information on corporate performance to be unlike anything else you have studied.

The engine that drives the highest levels of corporate performance is called Corporate Synergy. By now you should know that synergy is an extremely powerful and productive force. Unlike sexual synergy, most other forms of synergy exist upon a platform of *communication* and *goal setting*. For instance, consider a town that is being threatened by rising floodwaters. Synergy is able to occur because all of the townspeople share a *common goal*. They share a *common beacon*, which is to save their town! This causes the citizens to become "united" with one another. They become "indivisible." *They put aside their differences* and begin working together to save their town. They work endlessly, shoveling sand into bags and stacking

145

them into levees to hold back the water. They set up food stations, and volunteer their personal trucks and equipment to help move people's possessions to higher ground, regardless of whom those possessions belong to. They develop an *allegiance* to one another.

All of that may sound simple to the point of being obvious, but synergy is a valuable event in any process of success. That is why I have worked so hard to cleverly disguise it, particularly when it comes to business. For instance, have you seen those "Come join our team!" signs hanging everywhere? I've got half the companies in the United States currently believing that hanging a sign on the outside of their building somehow creates an environment of people productively working together. Well, sorry to have to tell you this, but hanging a little sign on the outside of a building doesn't exactly generate the impact of raging floodwaters.

Perhaps You Should All Wear Helmets

Over the years I have been able to convince a fair amount of business-people that comparing business with sports is a ridiculous proposition. If you happen to be one of those people, you are about to develop a new perspective.

For example, do you know the real beauty of a professional football team?

Wrong! It's not the cheerleaders.

The real beauty of a professional football team is the fact that every player has spent their *entire lives* training to be there. They have been focused on getting exactly where they are since they were children! They played peewee football, then grade school football, then junior high football, and then high school football followed by college football. Then, because they have become the absolute best in their field, they have achieved their life-long dream of playing in the pros.

How does that profile compare to the people who are currently working at your company right now? What about the people who are *managing* your company? How many of them have trained since they were children to have the exact jobs they have right now?

How many of them simply needed a job and responded to a classified ad?

Can you imagine the level of play within the National Football League if it selected its players from the Sunday want ads?

Do you still think business has nothing to learn from professional sports? Another lesson you can take from a professional sports team involves the hiring and placement of its players. A football team doesn't hire a grocery store manager to quickly fill a position in the offensive line. Wide receivers are not hired to play middle linebacker just because there was a position needing to be filled. Professional sports teams perform at a high level because they hire people who have trained for a lifetime, and then they place those people into the positions they have been training for. They place all the right people in all the right places. This is a model that transcends all team efforts. It is a model that any business could only hope to achieve. It is a model that *your* business should be trying to achieve.

The Intellectual Joining

of the Elbows

Not all lessons from sports paint wonderful pictures of success. For instance, not too long ago there was a professional football team that had a record *nine* Pro Bowl players on their team in the same year. For those of you who don't follow football, being selected as a Pro Bowl player distinguishes a player as being one of the absolute best at what he does. It is very similar to an actor or actress being nominated for an Oscar. For a team to have nine such players at the same time is very unusual. The team was considered to be *unstoppable*. But at the end of their 16-game season, they finished with a disappointing record of 3-wins and 13-losses!

Do you know why?

Because even though they had an abundance of individual talent, they couldn't play together as a team! The coaches thought they knew more than the players, the players thought they new more than the coaches, and some of the players thought they knew more than the other players. A lot of sports writers thought the team just had too much talent, but the only thing the team had too much of, was *arrogance.* The team had too many people thinking *they* knew more than the person next to them, and when that happens you don't have synergy, you have disease.

149

The team failed to do what many businesses are failing at right now. They had never had an Intellectual Joining of the Elbows, which I have worked very hard to prevent, and am going to work hard to repair right now.

Arrogance is one of my most effective tools in the war against synergy, so if you want your management team to begin performing at its highest level, you will need to bring an element of humbleness into the fold. In order for that to occur, there are a few things that need to happen.

The first thing you need to do is schedule a management meeting that will focus on "Team Building." Next, go out and collect three different styles of I.Q. tests. A variety of tests are important here because I.Q. tests tend to be heavily slanted toward mathematics. This obviously favors the math types and subsequently skews the results. Using three different varieties will help level the playing field.

Once you have all three tests, make as many copies of each as you have managers coming to attend the meeting. Next, create an overhead transparency to serve as an I.Q. score sheet. Be creative, and make sure the score sheet has the *name of each manager* that will be attending the meeting, and that it allows for and then divides, the total of all three scores, creating a final score.

Before the meeting, be sure there is an overhead projector in the meeting room. Check it to be sure it works and that there is a spare bulb on hand. Place the I.Q. score sheet on the projector, and then place a set of the three I.Q. tests face down in front of each chair in which a manager will be seated.

As the managers arrive be sure to acknowledge the documents that are placed in front of their chairs, and request that they be left face down until they come into play later in the meeting.

The first thing you need to mention in a team building meeting is the necessity of *mutual respect.* The Accounting Manager needs to be respected for his or her expertise in accounting. The Marketing Manager needs to be respected for his or her expertise in Marketing, and so on. It is essential that all the managers respect each other for the expertise they individually bring to the company, collectively forming the *key leadership team.*

Now for the intellectual joining of the elbows.

Urge the managers to recognize that it is not their *intelligence* that necessarily adds to the company's ability to perform, but their individual areas of expertise. Explain that they are more similar in intelligence than they may realize or even be willing to admit to. As a matter of fact, if they were to measure all of their I.Q.'s they would discover that their individual scores would most likely finish within +/- 5% of each other. A margin that thin could be swung by something as simple as a poor night's sleep, which takes away any bragging rights someone might think they have based on pure intellectual advantage.

Any *arrogant* managers you have will silently deny that's accurate; the *insecure* managers will silently hope that's accurate, and your *competent* managers will figure that is close to accurate.

At this point tell them that the company is determined to establish a common baseline from which to construct their newly revived commitment to leadership and teamwork, and for everyone's benefit, they are going to use intelligence as that baseline. Tell the managers that the company "believes that the opportunity to prove the intellectual similarity that exists among the managers will establish a common platform from which they can build upon, ultimately enhancing the collective ability of the team to perform."

At this point, call their attention to the documents that are lying face down in front of them. Explain that "great care" was given in selecting not one but *three* different I.Q. tests for them to complete. Let them know that it is to their advantage to be exposed to the liberal sampling of intellect that the three tests will provide.

By now the room will be filled with blank faces, and so quiet that the sound of a pin drop could shatter the face of a new Rolex wristwatch.

Now for the good part. Switch on the overhead projector, beaming up onto a large screen the I.Q. scoring sheet with *all* of their names appearing on it like a theatre marquee for a Hollywood movie premiere.

Explain that they will be given one hour to complete all three tests, being allotted twenty-minutes to complete each individual test. If they haven't finished the test they are current working on at the completion of twenty-minutes, they must move on. It is important for them to complete twenty minutes working in each of the three tests so that the benefit of liberal sampling can occur.

After one hour has elapsed they are to pass their tests to the person sitting next to them for scoring. After all the tests have been scored, everyone's scores will then be placed up on the screen.

Glance at your watch a few times as you explain that when the testing is over they will be pleasantly surprised at how similar their scores will be.

Now, stare at your watch while reminding them these are timed exams, then count it down, "Three... Two... One... STOP!"

Tell them to put their pencils down because they aren't actually going to take the tests.

You will be able to tell by the reaction in the room that the intellectual joining of the elbows has just occurred.

You have just swiftly and *dramatically* improved the teamwork potential of your management, bringing you one step closer to achieving corporate synergy.

When it comes to success in business, how smart you might think you are will only end up holding you back. Some managers might think they are smarter than the rest, but just like the football team with nine Pro Bowl players, these managers are only interfering with the management team's ability to perform. They are *inhibiting* more than *contributing,* and that's no way to win the game.

Robert Bakke

I.E.

It took getting where I am today to discover that the true intellectual separation that exists between humans is not I.Q., but a performance based attribute called I.E., which stands for "Interest Execution." This is something most of you have been referring to as, "Drive and Determination." In other words, what separates you is not necessarily something that can be tested for on a piece of paper. *What separates you are the individual interests that were placed within you prior to your birth.* These individual interests are what create your *drive* for knowledge in specific areas. This is why some students live, breathe and excel in auto-shop, while others spend all of their time in the biology lab.

Your *determination* is your ability to *execute performance* aligned with your interests. That is why people who are born with a strong I.E. for mathematics can do very well on an I.Q. test heavily loaded with math. This is also why no correlation can be found between I.Q. and acquired wealth. A self-made millionaire may score quite average on an I.Q. test because their I.E. is exceptionally strong in *marketing and business*, not algebra!

It is your I.E. that makes you different from each other, and at the same time, more valuable to each other. **A manager who thinks he or she is more intelligent and subsequently more valuable than the manager next to them is both inaccurate and unproductive.**

Managers who are humble are more inclined to show respect for their peers and the various areas of interest and expertise they bring to the team.

This creates a better team that will ultimately produce more successful and profitable results. That is why the Marketing manager must have respect for what the Accounting manager brings to the team, and the Accounting manager must have respect for what the Advertising manager brings to the team. While each of them brings about the same *amount* of knowledge, they bring different *types* of knowledge. That is what makes them so valuable to each other, whether they are in a conference room or on a playing field.

When members of a team don't have mutual respect for each other, the lineman doesn't carry out his blocking assignment, the running back gets tackled behind the line of scrimmage and the *entire team* loses.

"Top Secret" Company Goals

If you are a business owner, manager or employee and still don't believe I am influencing the way you do business, perhaps the following questions might cause you to ponder the subject.

Do you believe that being able to work together is important? Yes or No?

Do you believe it is important to set goals for your business? Yes or No?

Pretty obvious, correct?

Wow, you're good at this.

So why is it that most companies, including your own, continue to keep their goals such a secret? Isn't a "common" goal a goal that *everybody knows?* How can the employees of a company become "united" in the quest of the company if they haven't been told what the quest of the company, is?

Maybe that depends on what your definition of *is*, is. Whether you have ten employees or *ten thousand* employees, doesn't it make sense that they should all have a general knowledge of the company goals and an understanding of how their job is contributing toward the achievement of those goals? A well communicated company goal serves as a common beacon to help employees base their decisions upon and make their efforts toward. A company without a recognized goal in many respects is similar to a society without a recognized God. It deprives its people of a common beacon upon which to base their decisions, resulting in people going in every direction except the correct one.

If someone walked into the shipping area of your company and started asking employees what the Gross Annual Revenue target was for the current fiscal year, could anyone answer correctly?

What about the goal for total units sold? Would they know how many units were sold last month in comparison to this month? Do they know the number of units they must ship per day to satisfy customer expectations?

Companies want their employees to "take ownership" in their jobs, but if the employees don't know what they are working towards, how can they?

Look at this in terms of *synergy.*

Synergy doesn't occur just because you might have a thousand people working. Synergy occurs when you have a thousand people *working together toward a common goal.* If you want to produce *record profits*, you want to pay careful attention here.

Go back to the arena of professional sports. When playing against a given opponent, a football team has a target number of points, *a goal,* they know they need to score if they can expect to win. *Every player* knows this goal. The coaches put together a game plan to achieve this goal, and ensure every player knows this game plan. The game plan consists of individual plays designed for specific situations, and every player knows each of these plays. If the team needs to gain four yards, they run a play designed to achieve four yards. **Every player knows exactly what their individual role is in achieving the desired outcome.** If the players execute their individual assignments properly, synergy will occur and four yards will be achieved. This is the perfect example of people working together to achieve a common goal. Well, no it isn't. Bringing home the crew of Apollo 13 was the perfect example (currently available on video and DVD). Good football is a respectable second.

How does all of this compare to the business you are a part of right now? I would be willing to bet that less than ten-percent of the employees at your company actually know the goals of your company. If you think I'm kidding, just start asking them.

If you have a thousand employees at your company and only about ten percent of them know what the goals are, do you know what you have? You have less than one hundred employees working in the same direction, and more than *nine hundred* working in all directions! You can't expect employees to take ownership in a company that doesn't show them enough respect to include them in the direction and goals of the company!

Like I said before, you can have a thousand people working, or a thousand people working together toward a common goal. The choice is yours. But what do you suppose would happen on a football field only if one player knew the play?

Electronic Voice-Fail

If you don't want to be treated like wolves, avoid acting like pack animals. Just because other people are doing something doesn't mean you have to.

As you work to improve the communications at your company you will discover a very obvious and necessary change that needs to be made. It might seem like an illogical change because no one else is making it, but it is a change that will slowly bring you a competitive advantage. That change is this:

"You need to demonstrate your leadership, and go back to answering the telephone."

Do you remember any tales of the old west? If electronic communication was the weapon of the old quick-draw gunfighters, there would have been gunfighters hopping around all over with self-inflicted wounds to their feet!

Automated receptionists and voicemail systems were originally intended to be a convenient way to capture phone calls you might otherwise have missed. But thanks to me, today they have become something that alienates your customers who are looking to spend their money with you, and a convenient way to avoid other calls that might add to your workload.

Take a look at the big picture here. Out in the field, perhaps at a branch office or at one of your chain stores, a new employee has been hired. The new employee has a few specific and important questions on healthcare benefits. The questions are detailed to a point where the branch manager feels unable to adequately answer them. The branch manager tells the new employee that he or she will contact the Human Resources department at the corporate office, and have the answers momentarily. The manager attempts to contact the H.R. Director but the call goes straight into voicemail. That was on Monday.

On Tuesday the new employee seeks out their manager in hopes of learning the answers to their healthcare questions. The manager apologizes for not having the answers, and places another call to the H.R. Director. Again, the manager's call goes straight into voicemail. That was on Tuesday.

On Wednesday, the new employee again seeks answers, and again the manager apologizes and places a *third* call to the H.R. Director. The manager's call goes straight into voicemail, again!

On Thursday, the fourth day into this electronic event, the new employee's questions remain unanswered. The manager is frustrated and embarrassed, and the new employee is wondering what kind of rinky-dink backwater outfit they have gotten mixed up with.

Synergy? No way.

When it comes to voicemail, people know they should be returning calls as quickly as possible, particularly when it is a customer's call! Good business sense dictates that whenever you have been unavailable to accept calls, you should *immediately* check for missed calls and *return them* immediately. Even if you can't necessarily achieve resolution to the caller's inquiry you should at least be letting them know you've received their message and then provide them with a specific date that they can expect to be hearing from you again.

Sound logical?

Sound efficient?

Of course it does, but not as efficient as I am at preventing people from doing it.

Do you know why companies like electronic answering systems so much? It's because so many other companies are using them. It is a "pack" mentality that is costing *you* big money, and making *me* a fortune.

Do you honestly believe your customers would prefer to be greeted by a *machine* rather than a human being? If you believe that then you have a lot to learn about the social nature of human beings. Just take a drive down the highway and count the number of drivers talking on cellular telephones. This is an obvious clue I had to keep away from all those dot com'ers who thought that shoppers would flock to something that would ask for their credit card number without providing human social contact. Just because something allows employees to silently sneak off e-mails to their friends and buddies during the workday, and creates an unsecured way to bog down business communications with a new way to look busy, does not mean it will immediately change the shopping habits of the entire free world.

That crash might have padded my wallet, but it is *still* ringing in my ears!

Here is something else to ponder. Do you believe the great leaders of tomorrow will emerge as a result of hiding behind the safe-house of a computer monitor? **Or will they have the confidence to emerge from out behind their computer monitors and once again stand before people?**

After businesses have lost enough sales volume to automated receptionists and misused voicemail systems, businesses will once again greet customers with the warm and friendly voice of a real human being. Granted, new innovations have their place. But no single innovation can be all things for all applications. If you don't believe that, just take this little Golden Rule test. As quickly as you can, call your bank and ask the mortgage officer the current interest rate on a thirty year home loan, and how much you will save by paying off the loan fifteen years early. By the time you finish this little voicemail adventure *next week* you will be glad to pay some college kid $7.00 per hour to start answering the phone.

Maybe businesses should all consider taking a lesson from a futuristic cop flick entitled, "Demolition Man." In the movie, a police officer of the future answers the telephone and says, "San Angeles Police Department. If you would like the *automated* receptionist, press #1 now."

If you want to be a leader in the business world you have to gather as much information as possible and then make the decisions that make the most sense. Swinging way off in one direction or the other for the sole purpose of being one of the pack only makes sense if you are a wolf. Remember this, walking the middle ground gives you the best view in *both* directions, and everybody knows the 50-yard line is the best place to be. Everything else is just the cheap seats.

Ice Cream Money Management

This chapter is for younger humans only, so if you are an adult, "Press #1 now" and skip to the next chapter. (Annoying, isn't it?)

Another method that I have used to make a profound impact on your economy is the influencing of adult humans to...

Hey! I said if you are an adult, "Press #1 now" and skip to the next chapter! Reading this chapter will do to adults what country music did to the Martians in the movie, Mars Attacks! (Your heads will explode.) So bug out.

Okay young people, pay careful attention. Even when adults say they want to be responsible and conserve money, I can make them turn right around and spend as much money as they possible can. For example, this is how I've made many business managers, government workers and school administrators handle their budgets. This will sound crazy to you, but it is the truth! So you will just have to believe me.

Let's say a particular manager has a current annual budget of $100,000.00. As the end of the year approaches, the manager discovers that they will have only used $90,000.00 of their budget, leaving $10,000.00 left over.

That sounds like a good thing, correct? Well, not for long. Instead of *saving* the money, or even *investing* it until they need it later, the manager will go out and *intentionally* spend every last dime on whatever they can, even if it means buying several cases of #2 pencils just to throw in the closet and forget about. I am *not* kidding.

The problem is this. Midway through the current year, the manager had to present a new budget request for the upcoming year. That budget request was for $125,000.00 (a $25,000.00 increase above the current year). The manager will not receive the additional $25,000.00 for the upcoming year unless they can prove the need for it, which means spending *every penny* of the current year's budget! Basically, they will not receive $125, 000.00 for next year if they didn't spend the full $100,000.00 this year. Hence, they blow the remaining money on anything they can think of.

Year after year managers and administrators intentionally keep spending every dollar they can and asking for more and more, and more! Do you know why? Because everybody else is doing it! It's the human pack mentality, and that doesn't make it right.

Now you know the real reason why your taxes and college tuitions keep rising uncontrollably.

The odd part is, when the manager's next year's $125,000.00 budget request comes back approved in the amount of $120,000.00, the manager will complain that his or her "budget was cut." But in reality, they received a $20,000.00 increase above the current year's budget of $100,000.00 and $30,000.00 more than the $90,000.00 they actually needed. The increase from $90,0000.00 to $120,000.00 is a 33% increase, and yet they refer to it as a "cut." There are other, similar, "cut" scenarios.

Young humans need to know the truth about how many budgets are handled, and the terms budgets are discussed with, so they can enter the workforce with more practical and sound ways of handling money. Particularly if they end up working in the government.

Many government and state workers handle their budgets the same way, but with one big difference. Government employees *work for you*, because the money for their budgets and their paychecks comes directly out of *your* pocket. Unfortunately for you, they forget that, and commit dollars to spending plans that grow uncontrollably year after year. They get away with it right up to the point where the economy shrinks and reduces their income of tax dollars. This creates a budget *shortfall,* causing them to run completely out of money (ala 2002). No problem. They simply raise your taxes and take more of your money to cover their spending mistakes. What a deal. *They* make mistakes, and *you* pay for them.

Another interesting situation occurs when they end up with a budget *surplus.* This means the tax dollars they took from you ended up being more than they were able to spend. Some of *your money* was left over. Since they couldn't spend it all, they should return some of it back to you. After all, it is *your* money that you generated from *your* hard hours of labor, so shouldn't you get some of it back? A lot of people don't seem to think so.

Let's apply my little test of consistency to their logic.

If one of these government workers was at home and sent someone to a store to buy something for them, and the item cost less than the money they sent them to the store with, do you think they would expect to get their change back? You bet they would. But when they are spending *your* money they stop seeing it that way. They want *your* change, and if there is any left over, they believe they should be able to keep it.

I know some of this sounds crazy, but that's the way I've had the system working for many years now. It wasn't too difficult either. Apparently a lot of adults went to the Dairy Queen with Tom when they were kids.

This is a true story.

Tom and John wanted to go the Dairy Queen. They didn't have any money, so they asked John's mother if she could give them some. All she had was a five-dollar bill, but she gave it to them expecting there would be some money left over. John and Tom went to the Dairy Queen where they each purchased ice cream cones costing about $1.00 each. This left approximately $3.00 in change, which John put in his pocket with the intention of returning to his mother. Tom didn't see it that way. Tom argued that John's mother gave them $5.00 and that half of that money was his. He demanded that John give him his half of the change. John refused, and brought the $3.00 back to his mother.

Today, John runs his own business.

Tom works for the government.

I did not make this up.

Inside each of you is an inherent knowledge of right and wrong. Two soft little voices trying to move you in different directions. When spending other people's money, make sure you listen to the right voice.

One Nation Under... Who?

A couple last chapters on leadership. Successful leadership is fair, consistent, and serves justice in the course toward a recognized objective. It requires the ability to explore many sides of an issue while still retaining the ability to think for yourself. This can be difficult should you have allowed yourself to be swung too far in any one direction, which is often the result of being overly consumed by some kind of group affiliation. It takes a lot of confidence to be a part of a group and still have the intellectual strength to walk the spectrum and determine your own thoughts and opinions. As in the words of the famous general George Patton, who so accurately stated, "No one is thinking if everyone is thinking alike."

When you walk the entire spectrum of an issue you will find the best answers and solutions are usually found somewhere in the middle ground. Like a figure skater twirling in a perfectly balanced spin, as opposed to the thumping of a spin dryer after the clothes have been pulled too far to one side.

Keeping things off balance has been getting easier as the recognition of a Creator has been slowly removed from your society. Although I must admit, my efforts to keep you from pursuing the subject of a "God" are subtle compared to the efforts you are making by yourselves right now. One example of this would be the efforts that were made to rename your school system's "Christmas Vacation" to "Winter Break" so as not to offend non-Christians. That was one of *your* ideas. But when you think about it, since

America was founded upon a Christian God, and as long as *all the kids* got to have the time off from school, what difference did it make? Since Christmas vacation was a *pre-existing holiday,* is a part of *American tradition,* and because none of the kids were excluded, I'd say, "When in Rome, do as the Romans!" This is the kind of thing that is motivated by the same types who build a house next to an airport and then complain about aircraft noise. Besides, do you actually believe a blond-haired, blue-eyed American could move to Afghanistan and begin making changes to their Ramadan traditions? Not a chance. So, MERRY CHRISTMAS! Enjoy it!

My reasons for keeping your mind off of the Creator had nothing to do with the identical, cookie cutter treatment of humans that some of you are still trying to push onto other humans. My intentions, plain and simple, have been to prevent you from discovering the achievement potential that the Creator placed within you prior to your birth. And like I said before, unlike some of the trumpet blasting that goes on down there, my methods are subtle. For example, a very well known professional Top-Fuel drag racer named "Big Daddy" Don Garlits was competing in a national drag racing event. For those of you who don't know too much about him, Don (who has since retired and is now a broadcaster) was a 16-time World Champion. He drove a long, black Top-Fuel dragster, and was one of the greatest innovators of drag racing technology that the sport has ever known. For those of you who might be too young to remember, dragsters used to have engines in the front of the car. Today's rear engine dragsters were one of Don's many contributions to the sport.

One of the details about Don's car that you may not have known was that across the top of his long black dragster was a large white cross. Within the cross were the words, "God is love."

During one of his weekend racing events, Don and his team were having as many problems as a team could have. They were blowing up engines, breaking transmissions, you name it, and they were having problems with it. It was one of the team's worst weekends ever. But even with all the problems, Don and his team kept coming back to win round after round of elimination. They eventually went on to win the entire event, finishing in first place.

Immediately after Don's winning run, while still in his driver's suit and just after taking off his helmet, a television reporter was right there with a microphone.

The reporter asked: "Don, you faced every adversity imaginable this weekend but you hung in there and came away with the win. How did you do it?"

Don replied: "It was a rough weekend, but the Lord shined his light upon us, and I think what you have seen here today is a twentieth century miracle."

To that the reporter responds: "Will you be leaving for your next race right away, or taking a few days off to enjoy the win."

Subtle, to the point of *masterful*, don't you think?

Given Don's answer, the reporter could have very logically asked something about how Don felt his religious beliefs played a part in his victory, but I blanked that right out of the reporter's mind. I do that all the time, even still today. Just listen to the next sports interview where the subject of a God is mentioned. I'll blank that reporter's mind also, because it keeps your minds off of the Creator, and all of the talents and abilities he placed within you.

On the other hand, suppose Don would have replied to the reporter's question with an answer like, "We had a difficult weekend, but thanks to my new raccoon socks, we were able to pull off a win." In that case, the reporter would have been all over the subject of the raccoon socks, maybe to the point of starting a new fashion trend! But it wouldn't matter, because raccoon socks aren't going to put anyone into the winner's circle. But faith on the other hand, will put a checkered flag on your wall.

Bump & Slap

As the world continues to remove the recognition of a Creator from its daily events, humans slowly suffer the loss of a beacon for both direction and logic. That beacon-like quality can serve the people of a society very much the same as a common goal serves as a beacon for the employees of a company. **"When in doubt, do what will move you closer to the goal."** Without that, humans lose *consistency* in their logic, and begin basing their decisions on the trends of the times. This type of logic is typically small in scope, like a small framed picture hanging alone on a very large wall.

Great leaders think in very large pictures.

What is being emphasized is that a leader must be willing to consider multiple aspects of an issue, not just the convenient aspects or those aspects that are in political vogue. I am also emphasizing how political trends can swing a person's thoughts back and forth like the bump and slap of a windshield wiper, thereby interfering with the focus and consistency that an effective leader must have.

Let's look at an example. In fact, we'll use another example along the Christmas theme. Joy to the world. Ho, Ho, Ho... you get the idea.

Many travelers return home from European vacations and rave about Europe's culture and tradition, and then tiptoe around their own Christmas tradition with a politically correct, "Happy Holidays."

Well, which is it? Culture and tradition, or political correctness?

Food for thought. When someone offers you a Christmas greeting, or a Hanukah greeting, the *intent* of their message is, "I hope you have a great day!" How could any reasonable person who enjoys culture and tradition be offended by that?

Do you want to know the real definition of politically incorrect? Politically *incorrect* is when someone is greeted in the tradition of kindness and good will, but has been trained to find it offensive! *That* is politically incorrect! Some humans apparently have this backwards.

You must all work together to stop this trend. Besides, when you support a trend that takes away from your own Christmas tradition, you are not only supporting the subtle removal of a religious beacon from your society, but you are forgetting one other extremely important element.

Little humans absolutely adore Christmas!

How could anyone support a trend that will ultimately remove the smiles from the faces of children?

If it comes down to choosing between Santa, or *Scrooge*, I pick Santa! And so will your kids!

When an individual, a family, a business, or a society becomes void of a goal or beacon, they lose a consistent direction to their thoughts and actions. Their decisions become based on personal convenience and the trends of the time, ultimately slowing them down and preventing them from achieving their ultimate ambitions. That is why maintaining a goal or beacon in your life is so important. Goals keep you on course. They prevent you from swinging back and forth, right to left, bump and slap, wasting time and energy. Goals keep you on a truer, straighter course, ultimately bringing you to higher places. All great leaders know this.

Great leaders are consistent, fair, and able to *do the right thing* because they have a clear understanding of their objective. They are focused, and headed toward a beacon, which better enables them to maximize the talents, skills and abilities they were born with.

Now let's prove the existence of God, and let you get on with your day.

Believing in a God

That Cannot Be Seen

Trying to convince you that you were born with special gifts and abilities has one inherent flaw. If you don't believe in a spiritual existence, the entire concept that you were given assets of unlimited potential carries no merit. That means one of two things. I either stop trying to help you and head off to the links right now, or I convince you that the Creator himself, does in-fact exist.

Since I enjoy a good challenge, try as hard as you can to *not* believe what I am about to tell you.

Most of you resist the notion of a spiritual world because you refuse to believe in things you cannot see.

But have you ever seen an airplane flying overhead? You may not know this, but the wings of an airplane are designed to accelerate the air molecules that are passing over the top of the wings. These accelerated air molecules create an area of low pressure above the wing that literally sucks the airplane into the air. It is a process known as "lift."

Pilots can't actually "see" the lift, but for obvious reasons, they know that it is there.

You can prove this process for yourself by holding a piece of paper between your thumb and forefinger and draping the rest of the sheet over your hand. Blow across the top of the paper to accelerate the air molecules and the paper will rise. You will not be able to actually *see* the lift, but as the paper rises you too will know that it is there.

Speaking of air, it is the single most important life force on your planet, but can you actually *see* the air you are breathing?

What about the *temperature* of the air? If the air temperature increased by ten degrees could you *feel* the increase? Of course you could. But could you *see* the increase?

Suppose the temperature of the air was decreased by ten degrees. Could you *see* that?

Perhaps this will further prove my point. Open your hand and hold it up to your face. Now blow on it. Can you feel the air blowing against your skin? Can you *see* the air you are actually *feeling?*

Spooky, huh?

There are many things around you, including things that are keeping you alive at this moment that cannot be seen but most certainly exist.

Consider human potential. Consider *your own* potential. You cannot see it, but it is inside of you just as much as the air that is in your lungs. If you don't believe that, just blow on your hand a few more times.

Potential is an amazing asset when you believe in yourself enough to give it the breath of life, which is exactly what a couple of brothers from Ohio decided to do.

Orville and Wilbur Wright were just two ordinary little boys. Their mother having passed away, they lived alone with their father above his bicycle shop. They didn't have much money, but they did have a dream. They were determined to create the first successful flying machine. It didn't matter that they were being told time and again that it was impossible for humans to fly, because their *determination and potential* (both invisible to the naked eye), were far greater than the discouragement that was trying to keep

175

them down. Orville and Wilbur continued toward their goal, their beacon, until they had successfully created the world's first flying machine.

When the Wright brothers gave the breath of life to their potential, they created the groundwork for everything from today's commercial airliners to the space program. The very space program that brought you transistor radios, microwave ovens, the G.P.S. in your fishing boat and routine flights of a Space Shuttle that travels through the atmosphere at 18,000 miles per hour.

When you believe in the existence and the power of your potential it gives you the ability to achieve what others are intimidated to even try. If you won't believe me, perhaps you should believe the Wright brothers. However, if it is going to take something like a handshake from the Creator himself to finally get you to believe in your abilities, a handshake you will get.

Among so many other things the Creator has brought to the world, his greatest gift is the gift of love. Love is who he is. A reality so simple and clear that Don Garlits wrote it across the top of his dragster, and raced it to victory for all the world to see. So the question is, even though you can't *see* love, do you *believe* in love? More importantly, can you actually *feel* love? Of course you can, even though it too is invisible.

Have you ever felt the loss of a loved one? It *hurts* doesn't it? But why do you suppose it hurts the way it does? *It doesn't work to intellectualize it, because if grieving was caused by the mere knowledge of someone having passed, every time you saw an obituary in the morning paper you would cry tears into your coffee. But you don't, because it is not the mere knowledge of loss that causes you to suffer, it is the love you have for the person who has passed that causes you pain.*

The Creator is that love.

My words today may seem only that, but remember them vividly. For other, very painful days shall arrive to bring them new meaning. Days when tears will stream from the loss of a loved one now passed. It will be at that moment, while wrapped in a quilt of uncontrollable anguish, that you will look to the heavens and realize there is a power within you that is greater than all that is holding you back. An invisible power that is as real as the air that blows onto the palm of your hand.

Remember those words.

The Creator has given you the talents and abilities to conquer your fears and achieve the goals that *you know* are within you. It will be a tragedy, if it will take the pain of a loss, for you to finally believe in the love and the power who has given them to you. Ponder these words today, and with the rising of the new sun tomorrow, begin breathing life into that which is inside of you.

Robert Bakke

"Fore!"

Well, I guess that's it. I've done what I can to make amends for all of the wealth and intellect I have taken from the world. It's time for me to spend my weekdays at the golf course and Saturday nights at the racetrack (NASCAR is *huge* up here). And by the way, that new guy in the #3 car keeps winning everything!

So let's see. I have plenty of tees, my golf shoes are in my golf bag and... *nuts!* I need more golf balls. That's disappointing, because we can only play Titleist balls up here and they're *real* expensive. (Shipping charges I guess). Maybe I'll get lucky and the Pro Shop will be having a sale on ball retrievers.

So go have some fun today. ***Believe in your abilities. Encourage your children.*** Do this, and you will eventually achieve that bright red Ferrari of yours. Trust me on this, and maybe I'll see you when you get here.

178

About the Author

Robert Bakke is a black belt, a ski instructor, an aerobatic flight instructor, and was running a multi-million dollar company by the age of 24. During his business career, Robert managed sales of $1,000,000.00 to $3,000,000.00 *per day*, designed marketing programs that shattered existing sales records, and created business training programs that reduced management turnover by more than 50%. At the age of 30, Robert saluted good-bye to his business career, and moved on to captain jet aircraft, present public speaking and business training lectures, and author books to help people achieve their highest levels of performance.

Printed in the United States
24296LVS00002B/297